BEYOND BIRTH AND DEATH

BOOKS by
His Divine Grace A. C. Bhaktivedanta Swami Prabhupāda

Bhagavad-gītā As It Is
Śrīmad-Bhāgavatam (completed by disciples)
Śrī Caitanya-caritāmṛta
Kṛṣṇa, the Supreme Personality of Godhead
Teachings of Lord Caitanya
The Nectar of Devotion
The Nectar of Instruction
Śrī Īśopaniṣad
Light of the Bhāgavata
Easy Journey to Other Planets
Teachings of Lord Kapila, the Son of Devahūti
Teachings of Queen Kuntī
Message of Godhead
The Science of Self-Realization
The Perfection of Yoga
Beyond Birth and Death
On the Way to Kṛṣṇa
Rāja-vidyā: The King of Knowledge
Elevation to Kṛṣṇa Consciousness
Kṛṣṇa Consciousness: The Matchless Gift
Kṛṣṇa Consciousness: The Topmost Yoga System
Perfect Questions, Perfect Answers
Life Comes from Life
The Nārada-bhakti-sūtra (completed by disciples)
The Mukunda-mālā-stotra (completed by disciples)
Geetār-gān (Bengali)
Vairāgya-vidyā (Bengali)
Buddhi-yoga (Bengali)
Bhakti-ratna-boli (Bengali)
Back to Godhead magazine (founder)

BOOKS compiled from the teachings of
His Divine Grace A. C. Bhaktivedanta Swami Prabhupāda
after his lifetime

Search for Liberation
A Second Chance
The Journey of Self-Discovery
Civilization and Transcendence
The Laws of Nature
Renunciation Through Wisdom
The Quest for Enlightenment
Dharma, the Way of Transcendence
Beyond Illusion and Doubt
Bhakti-yoga: The Art of Eternal Love
Spiritual Yoga

BEYOND BIRTH AND DEATH

HIS DIVINE GRACE
A. C. Bhaktivedanta Swami Prabhupāda
Founder-Ācārya of the International Society for Krishna Consciousness

THE BHAKTIVEDANTA BOOK TRUST
Los Angeles • Stockholm • Mumbai • Sydney

Readers interested in the subject matter of this book are invited by the International Society for Krishna Consciousness to correspond with its secretary.

Beyond Birth and Death was prepared from transcripts of lectures Śrīla Prabhupāda gave in 1966 on the second and eighth chapters of the *Bhagavad-gītā*. The editor was Śrīla Prabhupāda's disciple Hayagrīva Dāsa (Howard Wheeler, M.A.).

International Society for Krishna Consciousness
P.O. Box 341445
Los Angeles, California 90034, USA
Telephone: 1-800-927-4152 (Inside USA);
1-310-837-5283 (Outside USA)
Fax: 1-310-837-1056
e-mail: bbt.usa@krishna.com
web: www.krishna.com

International Society for Krishna Consciousness
PO Box 380
Riverstone, NSW 2765, Australia
Phone: +61-2-9627-6306
Fax: +61-2-9627-6052
E-mail: bbt.au@krishna.com

Design: Arcita Dāsa

Cover Painting:
As the embodied soul continuously passes, in this body, from childhood to youth to old age, the soul similarly passes into another body at death.

Previous Printings: 250,000; This Printing, 2010: 100,000

Printed in Singapore

ISBN 0-912776-41-2

Contents

One

We Are Not These Bodies

dehī nityam avadhyo 'yaṁ
dehe sarvasya bhārata
tasmāt sarvāṇi bhūtāni
na tvaṁ śocitum arhasi

"O descendant of Bharata, he who dwells in the body can never be slain. Therefore you need not grieve for any living being." (*Bhagavad-gītā* 2.30)

The very first step in self-realization is realizing one's identity as separate from the body. "I am not this body but am spirit soul" is an essential realization for anyone who wants to transcend death and enter into the spiritual world beyond. It is not simply a matter of saying "I am not this body," but of actually realizing it. This is not as simple as it may seem at first. Although we are not these bodies but are pure consciousness, somehow or other we have become encased within the bodily dress. If we actually want the happiness and independence that transcend death, we have to establish ourselves and remain in our constitutional position as pure consciousness.

When we live in the bodily conception, our idea of happiness is like that of a man in delirium. Some philosophers claim that this delirious condition of bodily identification should be cured by abstaining from all action. Because material activities have been a source of distress for us, they claim that we should actually stop all activity. Their perfection is a kind of Buddhistic *nirvāṇa*, in which no activities are performed. Buddha maintained that the body has come into existence due to the combination of material elements and that if these material elements are somehow or other separated or dismantled, the cause of suffering will be removed. If the tax collector gives us too much difficulty because we happen to possess a large house, one simple solution is to destroy the house. But the *Bhagavad-gītā* indicates that the material body is not all in all. Beyond this combination of material elements there is spirit, and the symptom of that spirit is consciousness.

Consciousness cannot be denied. A body without consciousness is a dead body. As soon as consciousness is removed from the body, the mouth will not speak, the eyes will not see, and the ears will not hear. A child can understand that. It is a fact that consciousness is absolutely necessary for the animation of the body. What is this consciousness? Just as heat and light are symptoms of fire, so consciousness is the symptom of the soul. The energy of the soul, or self, is produced in the shape of consciousness. Indeed, consciousness proves that the soul is present. This is the conclusion not only of the *Bhagavad-gītā* but of all Vedic literature.

Both the impersonalistic followers of Śaṅkarācārya and the Vaiṣṇavas following in the disciplic succession from Lord Śrī Kṛṣṇa acknowledge the factual existence of the soul, but the Buddhist philosophers do not. The Buddhists contend that at a certain stage the combination of matter produces consciousness, but this argument is refuted by the fact that although we may have all the constituents of matter at our disposal, we cannot produce consciousness from them. All the material elements may be present in a dead man, but we cannot revive that man to consciousness. A man is not a machine. When a part of a machine breaks down, it can be replaced and the machine will work again, but when the body breaks down and consciousness leaves the body, there is no possibility of our replacing the broken part and reviving the body. The soul is different from the body, and as long as the soul is there, the body is animate. But there is no possibility of making the body animate in the absence of the soul.

Because we cannot perceive the soul with our gross senses, we deny that it exists. Actually, there are so many things we cannot see. We cannot see air, radio waves, or sound, nor can we perceive minute bacteria with our blunt senses, but this does not mean they are not there. With the aid of a microscope and other instruments, we can perceive many things previously unknown to those relying only on the imperfect senses. Just because the soul, which is atomic in size, has not been perceived yet with the blunt senses or instruments, we should not conclude that it is not there. We can, however, understand the presence of the soul by perceiving its symptoms and effects.

In the *Bhagavad-gītā* (2.14) Śrī Kṛṣṇa points out that all of our miseries are due to false identification with the body.

mātrā-sparśās tu kaunteya
śītoṣṇa-sukha-duḥkha-dāḥ
āgamāpāyino 'nityās
tāṁs titikṣasva bhārata

"O son of Kuntī, the nonpermanent appearance of happiness and distress, and their disappearance in due course, are like the appearance and disappearance of winter and summer seasons. They arise from sense perception, O scion of Bharata, and one must learn to tolerate them without being disturbed." In the summertime we may feel pleasure from contact with cold water, but in the winter we may shun that very water because it is too cold. In either case the water is the same, but we perceive it as pleasant or painful due to its contact with the body under different conditions.

All feelings of distress and happiness are due to the body. Under certain conditions the body and mind feel happiness or distress. Factually we are hankering after happiness, for the soul's constitutional position is that of happiness. The soul is part and parcel of the Supreme Being, who is *sac-cid-ānanda-vigrahaḥ*—the embodiment of eternity, knowledge, and bliss. Indeed, the very name Kṛṣṇa, which is nonsectarian, means "the greatest pleasure." *Kṛṣ* means "the greatest," and *ṇa* means "pleasure." Kṛṣṇa is the epitome of pleasure, and being part and parcel of Him, we hanker for pleasure. A drop of ocean water has all the properties of the ocean itself, and we, although minute particles of the Supreme Whole, have the same energetic properties as the Supreme.

The atomic soul, although so small, is moving the entire body to act in so many wonderful ways. In the world we see so many cities, highways, bridges, great buildings, monuments, and great civilizations, but who has done all this? It is all done by the minute spirit spark within the body. If such wonderful things can be performed by the minute spirit spark, we cannot begin to imagine what can be accomplished by the Supreme Spirit Whole. The natural hankering of the minute spirit spark is for the qualities of the whole— eternality, knowledge, and bliss—but these hankerings are being frustrated due to the material body. The information on how to attain the soul's desire is given in the *Bhagavad-gītā.*

At present we are trying to attain eternity, knowledge, and bliss by means of an imperfect instrument. Actually, our progress toward these goals is being blocked by the material body; therefore we have to come to the realization of our existence beyond the body. Theoretical knowledge that we are not these bodies will not do. We have to keep ourselves always separate as masters of the body, not as servants. If we know how to drive a car well, it will give us good service, but if we do not know how, we will be in danger.

The body is composed of senses, and the senses are always hungry after their objects. The eyes see a beautiful person and tell us, "Oh, there is a beautiful girl, a beautiful boy. Let's go see." The ears are telling us, "Oh, there is very nice music. Let us go hear it." The tongue is saying, "Oh, there is a very nice restaurant with palatable dishes. Let us go." In this way the senses are dragging us from one place to another, and because of this we are perplexed.

indriyāṇāṁ hi caratāṁ
yan mano 'nuvidhīyate
tad asya harati prajñāṁ
vāyur nāvam ivāmbhasi

"As a strong wind sweeps away a boat on the water, even one of the roaming senses on which the mind focuses can carry away a man's intelligence." (Bg. 2.67)

It is imperative that we learn how to control the senses. The name *gosvāmī* is given to someone who has learned how to master the senses. *Go* means "senses," and *svāmī* means "controller"; so one who can control the senses is to be considered a *gosvāmī.* Kṛṣṇa indicates that one who identifies with the illusory material body cannot establish himself in his proper identity as spirit soul. Bodily pleasure is flickering and intoxicating, and we cannot actually enjoy it, because of its momentary nature. Actual pleasure is of the soul, not the body. We have to mold our lives in such a way that we will not be diverted by bodily pleasure. If somehow we are diverted, it is not possible for us to establish our consciousness in its true identity beyond the body.

bhogaiśvarya-prasaktānāṁ
tayāpahṛta-cetasām
vyavasāyātmikā buddhiḥ
samādhau na vidhīyate

traiguṇya-viṣayā vedā
nistraiguṇyo bhavārjuna
nirdvandvo nitya-sattva-stho
niryoga-kṣema ātmavān

"In the minds of those who are too attached to sense enjoyment and material opulence, and who are bewildered by such things, the resolute determination for devotional service to the Supreme Lord does not take place. The *Vedas* deal mainly with the subject of the three modes of material nature. O Arjuna, become transcendental to these three modes. Be free from all dualities and from all anxieties for gain and safety, and be established in the self." (Bg. 2.44–45)

The word *veda* means "book of knowledge." There are many books of knowledge, which vary according to the country, population, environment, etc. In India the books of knowledge are referred to as the *Vedas.* In the West they are called the Old Testament and New Testament. The Muslims accept the Koran. What is the purpose for all these books of knowledge? They are to train us to understand our position as pure soul. Their purpose is to restrict bodily activities by certain rules and regulations, and these rules and regulations are known as codes of morality. The Bible, for instance, has ten commandments intended to regulate our lives. The body must be controlled in order for us to reach the highest perfection, and without regulative principles, it is not possible to perfect our lives. The regulative principles may differ from country to country or from scripture to scripture, but that doesn't matter, for they are made according to the time and circumstances and the mentality of the people. But the principle of regulated control is the same. Similarly, the government sets down certain regulations to be obeyed by its citizens. There is no possibility of making advancement in government or civilization without some regulations. In the second verse quoted above, Śrī Kṛṣṇa tells Arjuna that the regulative principles of the *Vedas* are primarily meant to control one's activities under the three modes of material nature—goodness, passion, and ignorance (*traiguṇya-viṣayā vedāḥ*). However, Kṛṣṇa is advising Arjuna to establish himself in his pure constitutional position as spirit soul, beyond the dualities of material nature.

As we have already pointed out, these dualities—such as heat and cold, pleasure and pain—arise due to the contact of the senses with their objects. In other words, they are born of identification with the body. Kṛṣṇa indicates that those who are devoted to enjoyment and power are carried away by the words of the *Vedas* that promise heavenly enjoyment by sacrifice and regulated activity. Enjoyment is our birthright, for it is the characteristic of the spirit soul, but when the spirit soul tries to enjoy materially, that is the mistake.

Everyone is turning to material subjects for enjoyment and is compiling as much knowledge as possible. Someone is becoming a chemist, physicist, politician, artist, or whatever. Everyone knows something of everything or everything of something, and this is generally known as knowledge. But as soon as we leave the body, all of this knowledge is vanquished. In a previous life one may have been a great man of knowledge, but in this life he has to start again by going to school and learning how to read and write from the beginning. Whatever knowledge was acquired in the previous life is forgotten. The situation is that we are actually seeking eternal knowledge, but this cannot be acquired by this material body.

We are all seeking enjoyment through these bodies, but bodily enjoyment is not our actual enjoyment. It is artificial. We have to understand that if we want to continue in this artificial enjoyment, we will not be able to attain our position of eternal enjoyment.

Identification with the body must be considered a diseased condition of the spirit soul. A diseased man cannot enjoy himself properly; a man with jaundice, for instance, will taste candy as bitter, but a healthy man can taste its sweetness. In either case the candy is the same, but according to our condition it tastes different. Unless we are cured of this diseased conception of bodily life, we cannot taste the sweetness of spiritual life. Indeed, it will taste bitter to us. At the same time, by increasing our enjoyment of material life, we are further complicating our diseased condition. A typhoid patient cannot eat solid food, and if someone gives it to him to enjoy and he eats it, he is further complicating his malady and is endangering his life. If we really want freedom from the miseries of material existence, we must minimize our bodily demands and pleasures.

Actually, material enjoyment is not enjoyment at all. Real enjoyment does not cease. In the *Padma Purāṇa* it is said, *ramante yogino 'nante:* the *yogīs* (*yogino*), those who are endeavoring to elevate themselves to the spiritual platform, are actually enjoying (*ramante*), but their enjoyment is *anante*, endless. This is because their enjoyment is in relation to the supreme enjoyer (Rāma), Śrī Kṛṣṇa. Bhagavān Śrī Kṛṣṇa is the real enjoyer, and in the *Bhagavad-gītā* (5.29) He confirms this:

bhoktāraṁ yajña-tapasāṁ
sarva-loka-maheśvaram
suhṛdaṁ sarva-bhūtānāṁ
jñātvā māṁ śāntim ṛcchati

"A person in full consciousness of Me, knowing Me to be the ultimate beneficiary of all sacrifices and austerities, the Supreme Lord of all planets and demigods, and the benefactor and well-wisher of all living entities, attains peace from the pangs of material miseries." *Bhoga* means "enjoyment," and our enjoyment comes from understanding our position as the enjoyed. The real enjoyer is the Supreme Lord, and we are enjoyed by Him.

An example of this relationship can be found in the material world between a husband and a wife: the husband is the enjoyer (*puruṣa*), and the wife is the enjoyed (*prakṛti*). The word *prakṛti* means "woman." *Puruṣa*, or spirit, is the subject, and *prakṛti*, or nature, is the object. The enjoyment, however, is participated in by both the husband and the wife. When actual enjoyment is there, there is no distinction that the husband is enjoying more or the wife is enjoying less. Although the male is the predominator and the female is the predominated, there is no division when it comes to enjoyment. On a larger scale, however, all living entities are *prakṛti* and are meant to be enjoyed by the Lord, the supreme *puruṣa*.

God expanded into many, and we constitute those expansions. God is one without a second, but He willed to become many in order to enjoy. We have experience that there is little or no enjoyment in sitting alone in a room talking to oneself. However, if there are five people present, our enjoyment is enhanced, and if we can discuss Kṛṣṇa before many, many people, the enjoyment is all the greater. Enjoyment means variety. God became many for His enjoyment, and thus our position is that of the enjoyed. That is our constitutional position and the purpose for our creation. Both enjoyer and enjoyed have consciousness, but the consciousness of the enjoyed is subordinate to the consciousness of the enjoyer. Although Kṛṣṇa is the enjoyer and we are the enjoyed, the enjoyment can be participated in equally by everyone. Our enjoyment can be perfected when we participate in the enjoyment of God. There is no possibility of our enjoying separately on the bodily platform. Material enjoyment on the gross bodily platform is discouraged throughout the *Bhagavad-gītā:*

mātrā-sparśās tu kaunteya
śītoṣṇa-sukha-duḥkha-dāḥ
āgamāpāyino 'nityās
tāṁs titikṣasva bhārata

"O son of Kuntī, the nonpermanent appearance of happiness and distress, and their disappearance in due course, are like the appearance and disappearance of winter and summer seasons. They arise from sense perception, O scion of Bharata, and one must learn to tolerate them without being disturbed." (Bg. 2.14)

The gross material body is a result of the interaction of the modes of material nature, and it is doomed to destruction.

antavanta ime dehā
nityasyoktāḥ śarīriṇaḥ
anāśino 'prameyasya
tasmād yudhyasva bhārata

"Only the material body of the indestructible, immeasurable, and eternal living entity is subject to destruction; therefore, fight, O descendant of Bharata." (Bg. 2.18) Śrī Kṛṣṇa therefore encourages us to transcend the bodily conception of existence and attain to our actual spiritual life.

guṇān etān atītya trīn
dehī deha-samudbhavān

janma-mṛtyu jarā-duḥkhair
vimukto 'mṛtam aśnute

"When the embodied being is able to transcend these three modes associated with the material body, he can become free from birth, death, old age, and their distresses and can enjoy nectar even in this life." (Bg. 14.20)

To establish ourselves on the pure spiritual platform (*brahma-bhūta*), above the three modes, we must take up the method of Kṛṣṇa consciousness. The gift of Caitanya Mahāprabhu, the chanting of the names of Kṛṣṇa—Hare Kṛṣṇa, Hare Kṛṣṇa, Kṛṣṇa Kṛṣṇa, Hare Hare/ Hare Rāma, Hare Rāma, Rāma Rāma, Hare Hare—facilitates this process. This method is called *bhakti-yoga* or *mantra-yoga*, and it is employed by the highest transcendentalists. How the transcendentalists realize their identity beyond birth and death, beyond the material body, and transfer themselves from the material universe to the spiritual universes are the subjects of the following chapters.

Two

Elevation at Death

There are different kinds of transcendentalists, who are called *yogīs*—*haṭha-yogīs, jñāna-yogīs, dhyāna-yogīs,* and *bhakti-yogīs*—and all of them are eligible to be transferred to the spiritual world. The word *yoga* means "to link up," and the *yoga* systems are meant to enable us to link with the transcendental world. As mentioned in the previous chapter, originally we are all connected to the Supreme Lord, but now we have been affected by material contamination. The process is that we have to return to the spiritual world, and that process of linking up is called *yoga*. Another meaning of the word *yoga* is "plus." At the present moment we are minus God, or minus the Supreme. When we add Kṛṣṇa—or God—to our lives, this human form of life becomes perfect.

At the time of death we have to finish that process of perfection. During our lifetime we have to practice the method of approaching that perfection so that at the time of death, when we have to give up this material body, that perfection can be realized.

prayāṇa-kāle manasācalena
bhaktyā yukto yoga-balena caiva
bhruvor madhye prāṇam āveśya samyak
sa taṁ paraṁ puruṣam upaiti divyam

"One who, at the time of death, fixes his life air between the eyebrows and, by the strength of *yoga*, with an undeviating mind, engages himself in remembering the Supreme Lord in full devotion, will certainly attain to the Supreme Personality of Godhead." (Bg. 8.10)

Just as a student studies a subject for four or five years and then takes his examination and receives a degree, similarly, with the subject of life, if we practice during our lives for the examination at the time of death, and if we pass the examination, we are transferred to the spiritual world. Our whole life is examined at the time of death.

yaṁ yaṁ vāpi smaran bhāvaṁ
tyajaty ante kalevaram
taṁ tam evaiti kaunteya
sadā tad-bhāva-bhāvitaḥ

"Whatever state of being one remembers when he quits his body, O son of Kuntī, that state he will attain without fail." (Bg. 8.6) There is a Bengali proverb that says that whatever one does for perfection will be tested at the time of his death. In the *Bhagavad-gītā* (8.11–12) Kṛṣṇa describes what one should do when giving up the body. For the *dhyāna-yogī* (meditator) Śrī Kṛṣṇa speaks the following verses:

yad akṣaraṁ veda-vido vadanti
viśanti yad yatayo vīta-rāgāḥ
yad icchanto brahmacaryaṁ caranti
tat te padaṁ saṅgraheṇa pravakṣye

sarva-dvārāṇi saṁyamya
mano hṛdi nirudhya ca
mūrdhny ādhāyātmanaḥ prāṇam
āsthito yoga-dhāraṇām

"Persons who are learned in the *Vedas,* who utter *oṁkāra,* and who are great sages in the renounced order enter into Brahman. Desiring such perfection, one practices celibacy. I shall now briefly explain to you this process by which one may attain salvation. The yogic situation is that of detachment from all sensual engagements. Closing all the doors of the senses and fixing the mind on the heart and the life air at the top of the head, one establishes himself in *yoga.*"

In the *yoga* system this process is called *pratyāhāra,* which means "just the opposite." Although during life the eyes are engaged in seeing worldly beauty, at death one has to retract the senses from their objects and see the beauty within. Similarly, the ears are accustomed to hearing so many sounds in the world, but at the moment of death one has to hear the transcendental *oṁkāra* from within.

oṁ ity ekākṣaraṁ brahma
vyāharan mām anusmaran
yaḥ prayāti tyajan dehaṁ
sa yāti paramāṁ gatim

"After being situated in this *yoga* practice and vibrating the sacred syllable *oṁ,* the supreme combination of letters, if one thinks of the Supreme Personality of Godhead and quits his body, he will certainly reach the spiritual planets." (Bg. 8.13) In this way, all the senses have to be stopped in their external activities and concentrated on the form of *viṣṇu-mūrti,* the form of God. The mind is very turbulent, but it has to be fixed on the Lord in the heart. When the mind is fixed within the heart and the life air is transferred to the top of the head, one can attain perfection in *yoga.*

At this point the *yogī* determines where he is to go. In the material universe there are innumerable planets, and beyond this universe there is the spiritual universe. The *yogīs* have information of these places from the Vedic literatures. Just as someone planning to go to America can get some idea what the country is like by reading books, one can also have knowledge of the spiritual planets by reading the Vedic literatures. The *yogī* knows all these descriptions, and he can transfer himself to any planet he likes, without the help of spaceships. Space travel by mechanical means is not the accepted process for elevation to other planets. Perhaps with a great deal of time, effort, and money a few men may be able to reach other planets by material means—spaceships, space suits, etc.—but this is a very cumbersome and impractical method. In any case, it is not possible to go beyond the material universe by mechanical means.

The generally accepted method for transferal to higher planets is the practice of the meditational *yoga* system or *jñāna* system. The *bhakti-yoga* system, however, is not to be practiced for transferal to any material planet. Those who are servants of Kṛṣṇa, the Supreme Lord, are not interested in any planets in this material world because they know that on whatever planet one enters in the material sky, the four principles of birth, old age, disease, and death are present. On higher planets, the duration of life may be longer than on this earth, but death is there nonetheless. By "material universe" we refer to those planets where birth, old age, disease, and death reside, and by "spiritual universe" we refer to those planets where there is no birth, old age, disease, or death. Those who are intelligent do not try to elevate themselves to any planet within the material universe.

If one tries to enter higher planets by mechanical means, instant death is assured, for the body cannot stand the radical changes in atmosphere. But if one attempts to go to higher planets by means of the *yoga* system, he will acquire a suitable body for entrance. We can see this demonstrated on this earth, for we know it is not possible for us to live in the sea, in a watery atmosphere, nor is it possible for aquatics to live on the land. As we understand that even on this planet one has to have a particular type of body to live in a particular place, so a particular type of body is required for other planets. On the higher planets, bodies live much longer than on earth, because six months on earth is equal to one day on the higher planets. Thus the *Vedas* describe that those who live on the higher planets live for up to ten thousand earth years. Yet despite such a long life span, death awaits everyone. Even if one lives for twenty thousand or fifty thousand or even ten millions years, in the material world the years are all counted, and death is there. How can we escape this subjugation by death? That is the lesson of the *Bhagavad-gītā*.

na jāyate mriyate vā kadācin
nāyaṁ bhūtvā bhavitā vā na bhūyaḥ
ajo nityaḥ śāśvato 'yaṁ purāṇo
na hanyate hanyamāne śarīre

"For the soul there is neither birth nor death at any time. He has not come into being, does not come into being, and will not come into being. He is unborn, eternal, ever-existing, and primeval. He is not slain when the body is slain." (Bg. 2.20)

We are spirit soul, and as such we are eternal. Why, then, should we subject ourselves to birth and death? One who asks this question is to be considered intelligent. Those who are Kṛṣṇa conscious are very intelligent because they are not interested in gaining entrance to any planet where there is death. They will reject a long duration of life in order to attain a body like God's. *Īśvaraḥ paramaḥ kṛṣṇaḥ sac-cid-ānanda-vigrahaḥ*. *Sat* means "eternal," *cit* means "full of knowledge," and *ānanda* means "full of pleasure." Kṛṣṇa is the reservoir of all pleasure. If we transfer ourselves from this body into the spiritual world—either to Kṛṣṇaloka (Kṛṣṇa's planet) or any other spiritual planet—we will receive a similar *sac-cid-ānanda* body. Thus the aim of those who are in Kṛṣṇa consciousness is different from the aim of those who are trying to promote themselves to higher planets within this material world.

The self, or soul, of the individual is a minute spiritual spark. The perfection of *yoga* lies in the transferal of this spiritual spark to the top of the head. Having attained this, the *yogī* can transfer himself to any planet in the material world, according to his desire. If the *yogī* is curious to know what the moon is like, he can transfer himself there, or if he is interested in higher planets, he can transfer himself there, just as travelers go to New York, London, or other cities on the earth. Wherever one goes on earth, he finds the same visa and customs systems operating, and on all the material planets one can similarly see the principles of birth, old age, disease, and death operating.

Oṁ ity ekākṣaraṁ brahma: at the point of death the *yogī* can pronounce *oṁ, oṁkāra,* the concise form of transcendental sound vibration. If the *yogī* can vibrate this sound and at the same time remember Kṛṣṇa, or Viṣṇu (*mām anusmaran*), he attains the highest goal. The purpose of *yoga* is to concentrate the mind on Viṣṇu. The impersonalists imagine some form of the Supreme Lord, but the personalists do not imagine this: they actually see. Whether one imagines Him or actually sees Him, one has to concentrate his mind on the personal form of Kṛṣṇa.

ananya-cetāḥ satataṁ
yo māṁ smarati nityaśaḥ
tasyāhaṁ sulabhaḥ pārtha
nitya-yuktasya yoginaḥ

"For one who always remembers Me without deviation, I am easy to obtain, O son of Pṛthā, because of his constant engagement in devotional service." (Bg. 8.14)

Those who are satisfied with temporary life, temporary pleasure, and temporary facilities are not intelligent, at least not according to the *Bhagavad-gītā*. According to the *Gītā*, one whose brain substance is very meager is interested in temporary things. We are eternal, so why should we be interested in temporary things? No one wants a nonpermanent situation. If we are living in an apartment and the landlord asks us to vacate, we are sorry, but we are not sorry if we move into a better apartment. Because we are permanent, it is our nature to want a permanent residence. We don't wish to die, because in actuality we are permanent. Nor do we want to grow old or be diseased, because these are all external or nonpermanent states. Although we are not meant to suffer from fever, sometimes fever comes, and we have to take precautions and remedies to get well again. The fourfold miseries are like a fever, and they are all due to the material body. If somehow we can get out of the material body, we can escape the miseries that are integral to it.

For the impersonalists to get out of this temporary body, Kṛṣṇa here advises that they vibrate the syllable *oṁ*. In this way they can be assured of transmigration to the spiritual world. However, although they may enter the spiritual world, they cannot enter any of the planets there. They remain outside, in the *brahmajyoti*. The *brahmajyoti* may be compared to the sunshine, and the spiritual planets may be compared to the sun itself. In the spiritual sky the impersonalists remain in the effulgence of the Supreme Lord, the *brahmajyoti*. The impersonalists are placed in the *brahmajyoti* as spiritual sparks, and in this way the *brahmajyoti* is filled with spiritual sparks. This is what is meant by merging into the spiritual existence.

It should not be considered that one merges into the *brahmajyoti* in the sense of becoming one with it; the individuality of the spiritual spark is retained, but because the impersonalist does not want to take a personal form, he remains as a spiritual spark in that effulgence. Just as the sunshine is composed of so many atomic particles, so the *brahmajyoti* is composed of so many spiritual sparks.

However, as living entities we want enjoyment. Being, in itself, is not enough. We want bliss (*ānanda*) as well as being (*sat*). In his entirety, the living entity is composed of three qualities—eternality, knowledge, and bliss. Those who enter impersonally into the *brahmajyoti* can remain there for some time in full knowledge that they are now merged homogeneously with Brahman, but they cannot have that eternal *ānanda,* bliss, because that part is wanting. One may remain alone in a room for some time and may enjoy himself by reading a book or engaging in some thought, but it is not possible to remain in that room for years and years at a time, and certainly not for all eternity. Therefore, for one who merges impersonally into the existence of the Supreme, there is every chance of falling down again into the material world in order to acquire some association. This is the verdict of *Śrīmad-Bhāgavatam.* Astronauts may travel thousands and thousands of miles, but if they do not find rest on some planet, they have to return to earth. In any case, rest is required. In the impersonal form, rest is uncertain. Therefore *Śrīmad-Bhāgavatam* says that even after so much endeavor, if the impersonalist enters the spiritual world and acquires an impersonal form, he returns again to the material world because of neglecting to serve the Supreme Lord in love and devotion. As long as we are here on earth, we must learn to practice to love and serve Kṛṣṇa, the Supreme Lord. If we learn this, we can enter those spiritual planets. The impersonalist's position in the spiritual world is nonpermanent, for out of loneliness he will attempt to acquire some association. Because he does not associate personally with the Supreme Lord, he has to return to the material world and associate with conditioned living entities there.

It is of utmost importance, therefore, that we know the nature of our constitutional position: we want eternity, complete knowledge, and also pleasure. When we are left alone for a long time in the impersonal *brahmajyoti,* we cannot have pleasure, and therefore we accept the pleasure given by the material world. But in Kṛṣṇa consciousness, real pleasure is enjoyed. In the material world it is generally accepted that the highest pleasure is sex. This is a perverted reflection of the sex pleasure in the spiritual world. But we should not think that the pleasure there is like the sex pleasure in the material world. No, it is different. But unless sex is there in the spiritual world, it cannot be reflected here. Here it is simply a perverted reflection, but the actual life is there in Kṛṣṇa, who is full of all pleasure. Therefore, the best process is to train ourselves now, so that at the time of death we may transfer ourselves to the spiritual universe, to Kṛṣṇaloka, and there enjoy in the association of Kṛṣṇa. In the *Brahma-saṁhitā* (5.29) Śrī Kṛṣṇa and His abode are described thus:

cintāmaṇi-prakara-sadmasu kalpa-vṛkṣa-
lakṣāvṛteṣu surabhīr abhipālayantam
lakṣmī-sahasra-śata-sambhrama-sevyamānaṁ
govindam ādi-puruṣaṁ tam ahaṁ bhajāmi

"I worship Govinda, the primeval Lord, the first progenitor, who is tending cows yielding all desires in abodes built with spiritual gems and surrounded by millions of purpose trees. He is always served with great reverence and affection by hundreds and thousands of goddesses of fortune." This is a description of Kṛṣṇaloka. The houses are made of what is called "touchstone." Whatever touchstone touches immediately turns into gold. The trees are wish-fulfilling trees, or "desire trees," for one can receive from them whatever he wishes. In this world we get mangoes from mango trees and apples from apple trees, but there from any tree one can get whatever he desires. Similarly, the cows are called *surabhi*, and they yield an endless supply of milk. These descriptions of the spiritual planets are found in Vedic scriptures.

In this material world we have become acclimatized to birth, death, old age, and disease. Material scientists have discovered many facilities for sense enjoyment and destruction, but they have discovered no solution to the problems of birth, death, old age, and disease. They cannot make any machine that will check birth, death, old age, or disease. We can manufacture something that will accelerate death, but nothing that will stop death. Those who are intelligent, however, are concerned not with these four miseries of material life but with elevation to the spiritual planets. One who is continuously in trance (*nitya-yuktasya yoginaḥ*) does not divert his attention to anything else. His mind is always filled with the thought of Kṛṣṇa, without deviation (*ananya-cetāḥ satatam yo māṁ smarati nityaśaḥ*). *Satatam* refers to anywhere and any time.

In India I lived in Vṛndāvana, and now I am in America, but this does not mean that I am out of Vṛndāvana, because if I think of Kṛṣṇa always, then I'm always in Vṛndāvana, regardless of my material location. Kṛṣṇa consciousness means that one always lives with Kṛṣṇa on His spiritual planet, Goloka Vṛndāvana, and that one is simply waiting to give up this material body. *Smarati nityaśaḥ* means "continuously remembering," and for one who is continuously remembering Kṛṣṇa, the Lord becomes *sulabhaḥ*—easily purchased. Kṛṣṇa

Himself says that He is easily purchased by this *bhakti-yoga* process. Then why should we take to any other process? We can chant Hare Kṛṣṇa, Hare Kṛṣṇa, Kṛṣṇa Kṛṣṇa, Hare Hare/ Hare Rāma, Hare Rāma, Rāma Rāma, Hare Hare twenty-four hours daily. There are no rules and regulations. One can chant in the street, in the subway, or at his home or office. There is no tax and no expense. So why not take to it?

Three

Liberation from the Material Planets

The *jñānīs* and *yogīs* are generally impersonalists, and although they attain the temporary form of liberation by merging into the impersonal effulgence, the spiritual sky, according to *Śrīmad-Bhāgavatam* their knowledge is not considered pure. By penances, austerities, and meditations they can rise up to the platform of the Supreme Absolute, but as has been explained, they fall down to the material world because they have not taken Kṛṣṇa's personal features seriously. Unless one worships the lotus feet of Kṛṣṇa, he has to descend to the material platform. The ideal attitude should be, "I am Your eternal servitor. Please let me somehow engage in Your service." Kṛṣṇa is called *ajita*—unconquerable—for no one can conquer God, but according to *Śrīmad-Bhāgavatam*, one with this attitude easily conquers the Supreme. *Śrīmad-Bhāgavatam* also recommends that we give up the futile attempt to measure the Supreme. We cannot even measure the limitations of space, what to speak of the Supreme. It is not possible to measure the length and breadth of Kṛṣṇa by one's minuscule knowledge, and one who arrives at this conclusion is considered intelligent by the Vedic literature. One should come to understand, submissively, that he is a very insignificant segment of the universe. Abandoning the endeavor to understand the Supreme by our limited knowledge or mental speculation, we should become submissive and hear of the Supreme from the lips of a realized soul, or from such authoritative sources as the *Bhagavad-gītā*.

In the *Bhagavad-gītā* Arjuna is hearing about God from the lips of Śrī Kṛṣṇa Himself. In this way Arjuna set the criterion for understanding the Supreme by submissive hearing. It is our position to hear the *Bhagavad-gītā* from the lips of Arjuna or his bona fide representative, the spiritual master. After hearing, it is necessary to practice this acquired knowledge in daily life. "My dear Lord, You are unconquerable," the devotee prays, "but by this process, by hearing, You are conquered." God is unconquerable, but He is conquered by the devotee who abandons mental speculation and listens to authoritative sources.

According to the *Brahma-saṁhitā*, there are two ways of acquiring knowledge: the ascending process and the descending process. By the ascending process one is elevated by knowledge he himself acquires. In this way one thinks, "I don't care for any authorities or books. I'll learn about God on my own. I'll meditate and philosophize, and in this way I'll understand God." The other process, the descending process, involves receiving knowledge from higher authorities. The *Brahma-saṁhitā* states that if one takes to the ascending process and travels at the speed of mind and wind for millions of years, he will still end up not knowing God. For him, the subject matter will remain elusive and inconceivable. But the simple process for understanding that subject matter is given in the *Bhagavad-gītā: ananya-cetāḥ satataṁ yo māṁ smarati nityaśaḥ*. Kṛṣṇa says to meditate on Him without deviating from the path of devotional service in submission. For one who worships Him in this way, *tasyāhaṁ sulabhaḥ:* "I become easily available." This is the process: if one works for Kṛṣṇa twenty-four hours a day, Kṛṣṇa cannot forget him. By becoming submissive, he can attract the attention of God. As my Guru Mahārāja used to say, "Don't try to see God. Is God to come and stand before us like a servant just because we want to see Him? That is not the submissive way. We have to oblige Him by our love and service."

The proper process for approaching Kṛṣṇa was given to humanity by Lord Caitanya Mahāprabhu, and Rūpa Gosvāmī, His first disciple, appreciated it. Rūpa Gosvāmī was a minister in the Muhammadan government, but he left the government to become a disciple of Caitanya Mahāprabhu. When he first went to see the Lord, Rūpa Gosvāmī approached Him with the following verse:

namo mahā-vadānyāya
kṛṣṇa-prema-pradāya te
kṛṣṇāya kṛṣṇa-caitanya-
nāmne gaura-tviṣe namaḥ

"I offer my respectful obeisances unto the Supreme Lord, Śrī Kṛṣṇa Caitanya, who is more munificent than any other *avatāra*, even Kṛṣṇa Himself, because He is bestowing freely what no one else has ever given—pure love of Kṛṣṇa."

Kṛṣṇa gives Himself to one who attains pure love for Him. So Rūpa Gosvāmī called Caitanya Mahāprabhu the most munificent personality because He was offering the most precious thing of all very cheaply—Kṛṣṇa. We are all hankering after Kṛṣṇa because He is the most attractive, the most beautiful, the most opulent, the most powerful, and the most learned. Kṛṣṇa is the reservoir of all of this; so we need only turn our attention toward Him, and we will get everything. Everything—whatever we want. Whatever is our heart's desire will be fulfilled by this process of Kṛṣṇa consciousness.

As stated before, for one who dies in Kṛṣṇa consciousness, entrance into Kṛṣṇaloka, the supreme abode where Kṛṣṇa resides, is guaranteed. At this point one may ask what the advantage is in going to that planet, and Kṛṣṇa Himself answers:

mām upetya punar janma
duḥkhālayam aśāśvatam
nāpnuvanti mahātmānaḥ
saṁsiddhiṁ paramāṁ gatāḥ

"After attaining Me, the great souls, who are *yogīs* in devotion, never return to this temporary world, which is full of miseries, because they have attained the highest perfection." (Bg. 8.15) This material world is certified by Śrī Kṛṣṇa, the creator, as *duḥkhālayam*—full of miseries. How then can we make it comfortable? Is it possible to make this world comfortable by the so-called advancement of science? No, this is not possible. As a result, we do not even wish to know what these miseries are. The miseries, as stated before, are birth, old age, disease, and death, and because we cannot make a solution to them, we try to set them aside. Science has no power to solve these miseries, which are always giving us trouble. Instead, the scientists divert their attention to the making of spaceships or atomic bombs.

The solution to these problems is given in the *Bhagavad-gītā:* one who attains to Kṛṣṇa's platform does not have to return to this world of birth and death. We should try to understand that this place is full of miseries. It takes a certain amount of developed consciousness to understand this. Cats and dogs and hogs cannot understand that they are suffering. Man is called a rational animal, but his rationality is being used to further his animalistic propensities instead of to find out how to get liberation from this miserable condition. Here Kṛṣṇa explicitly states that one who comes to Him will never be reborn to suffer miseries again. Those great souls who come

His Divine Grace
A. C. Bhaktivedanta Swami Prabhupāda
Founder-*ācārya* of the International Society for Krishna Consciousness

PLATE 1 "As a strong wind sweeps away a boat on the water, even one of the roaming senses on which the mind focuses can carry away a man's intelligence." The horses represent the five senses, the reins symbolize the mind, the driver stands for the intelligence, and the passenger represents the spirit soul. (p. 5)

PLATE 2 If the *yogī* is curious to know what the moon is like, he can transfer himself there, or if he is interested in higher planets, he can transfer himself there, just as travelers go to New York, London, or other cities on the earth. (p. 17)

PLATE 3 At the end of a day of Brahmā, all the lower planetary systems are covered with water, and the beings on them are annihilated. (p. 31)

PLATE 4 This whole material universe is like a small, insignificant cloud in the vast spiritual sky. This material universe is encased by the *mahat-tattva*, matter. As a cloud has a beginning and an end, this material nature also has a beginning and an end. (p. 33)

PLATE 5 To establish ourselves on the pure spiritual platform, we must take up the method of Kṛṣṇa consciousness. The gift of Caitanya Mahāprabhu, the chanting of the names of Kṛṣṇa—Hare Kṛṣṇa, Hare Kṛṣṇa, Kṛṣṇa Kṛṣṇa, Hare Hare/ Hare Rāma, Hare Rāma, Rāma Rāma, Hare Hare—facilitates this process. (p. 11)

PLATE 6 Kṛṣṇa is the most attractive, the most beautiful, the most opulent, the most powerful, and the most learned. Kṛṣṇa is the reservoir of all of this; so we need only turn our attention toward Him, and we will get everything. (p. 25)

PLATE 7 The purpose of all Vedic instructions is to achieve the ultimate goal of life—to go back to Godhead. All indications for the satisfaction of our soul's innermost desires point to those worlds of Kṛṣṇa beyond birth and death. (pp 48–49)

to Him have attained the highest perfection of life, which alleviates the living entity from the suffering of conditioned existence.

One of the differences between Kṛṣṇa and an ordinary being is that an ordinary entity can be in only one place at a time but Kṛṣṇa can be everywhere in the universe and yet also in His own abode, simultaneously. Kṛṣṇa's abode in the transcendental kingdom is called Goloka Vṛndāvana. The Vṛndāvana in India is that same Vṛndāvana descended to this earth. When Kṛṣṇa descends by His own internal potency, His *dhāma,* or abode, also descends. In other words, when Kṛṣṇa descends to this earth, He manifests Himself in that particular land. Despite this, Kṛṣṇa's abode remains eternally in the transcendental sphere, in the Vaikuṇṭhas. In this verse Kṛṣṇa proclaims that one who comes to His abode in the Vaikuṇṭhas never has to take birth again in the material world. Such a person is called a *mahātmā.* The word *mahātmā* is generally heard in the West in connection with Mahatma Gandhi, but we should understand that *mahātmā* is not the title of a politician. Rather, *mahātmā* refers to the first-class Kṛṣṇa conscious man who is eligible to enter into the abode of Kṛṣṇa. The *mahātmā's* perfection is this: to utilize the human form of life and the resources of nature to extricate himself from the cycle of birth and death.

An intelligent person thinks, "I do not want miseries, but they are inflicted upon me by force. Why?" As stated before, we are always in a miserable condition due to disturbances arising from our mind and body, nature, or other living entities. There is always some kind of misery being inflicted upon us. This material world is meant for misery; unless the misery is there, we cannot come to Kṛṣṇa consciousness. Miseries actually help elevate us to Kṛṣṇa consciousness. An intelligent man questions why these miseries are inflicted on him by force.

However, modern civilization's attitude is "Let me cover my suffering with some intoxication, that's all." But as soon as the intoxication is over, the miseries return. It is not possible to make a solution to the miseries of life by artificial intoxication. The solution is Kṛṣṇa consciousness.

One may point out that although the devotees of Kṛṣṇa are trying to enter Kṛṣṇa's planet, everyone else is interested in going to the moon. Isn't going to the moon also perfection? The tendency to travel to other planets is always present in the living entity. One name for the living entity is *sarva-gata*, which means "one who wants to travel everywhere." Travel is part of the nature of the living entity. The desire to go to the moon is not a new thing. The *yogīs* are also interested in entering the higher planets, but in the *Bhagavad-gītā* (8.16) Kṛṣṇa points out that this will not be of any help.

ā-brahma-bhuvanāl lokāḥ
punar āvartino 'rjuna
mām upetya tu kaunteya
punar janma na vidyate

"From the highest planet in the material world down to the lowest, all are places of misery wherein repeated birth and death take place. But one who attains to My abode, O son of Kuntī, never takes birth again." The universe is divided into higher, middle, and lower planetary systems. The earth is considered to be a member of the middle planetary system. Kṛṣṇa points out that even if one enters into the highest planet of all, called Brahmaloka, there is still repetition of birth and death. Other planets in the universe are full of living entities. We should not think that here on earth there are living entities but all the other planets are vacant. From experience we can see that no place on earth is vacant, without living entities. If we dig deep down into the earth, we find worms; if we go deep into the water, we find aquatics; if we go into the sky, we find so many birds. How is it possible to conclude that other planets have no living entities? But Kṛṣṇa points out that even if we enter into those planets where great demigods reside, we will still be subjected to death. Here Kṛṣṇa repeats that upon reaching His planet one need not take birth again. We should be very serious about attaining our eternal life, full of bliss and knowledge. We have forgotten that this is actually our aim of life, our real self-interest. Why have we forgotten? We have simply been entrapped by the material glitter—by skyscrapers, big factories, politics—although we know that however big we build skyscrapers, we will not be able to live here forever. We should not spoil our energy in building mighty industries and cities to further entrap ourselves in material nature. Rather, we should use our energy to develop Kṛṣṇa consciousness so that after leaving this body we can enter Kṛṣṇa's spiritual planet. Kṛṣṇa consciousness is not a religious formula or some spiritual recreation; it is the most important thing in our lives.

Four

The Sky Beyond the Universe

If even those on the higher planets in this universe are subject to birth and death, why do great *yogīs* strive for elevation to them? Although they may have many mystic powers, these *yogīs* still have the tendency to enjoy the facilities of material life. On the higher planets, it is possible to live for incredibly long lifetimes. The time calculation on these planets is indicated by Śrī Kṛṣṇa in the *Bhagavad-gītā* (8.17):

sahasra-yuga-paryantam
ahar yad brahmaṇo viduḥ
rātriṁ yuga-sahasrāntāṁ
te 'ho-rātra-vido janāḥ

"By human calculation, a thousand ages taken together form the duration of Brahmā's one day. And such also is the duration of his night."

One *yuga* covers 4,320,000 years. This number multiplied by one thousand is calculated to be the twelve hours of Brahmā's daytime on the planet Brahmaloka. Similarly, another twelve-hour period covers the night. Thirty such days equal a month, twelve months equal a year, and Brahmā lives for one hundred such years. Life on such a planet is indeed long, yet even after trillions of years, the inhabitants of Brahmaloka have to face death. Unless we go to the spiritual planets, there is no escape from death.

avyaktād vyaktayaḥ sarvāḥ
prabhavanty ahar-āgame
rātry-āgame pralīyante
tatraivāvyakta-saṁjñake

"At the beginning of Brahmā's day, all living entities become manifest from the unmanifest state, and thereafter, when the night falls, they are merged into the unmanifest again." (Bg. 8.18)

At the end of a day of Brahmā, all the lower planetary systems are covered with water, and the beings on them are annihilated. After this devastation, and after the night of Brahmā passes, in the morning when Brahmā arises there is again creation, and all these beings come forth. Thus subjection to creation and destruction is the nature of the material world.

bhūta-grāmaḥ sa evāyaṁ
bhūtvā bhūtvā pralīyate
rātry-āgame 'vaśaḥ pārtha
prabhavaty ahar-āgame

"Again and again, when Brahmā's day arrives, all living entities come into being, and with the arrival of Brahmā's night, O Pārtha, they are helplessly annihilated." (Bg. 8.19) Although the living entities do not like devastation, that devastation will come and overflood the planets until all living beings on the planets stay merged in water throughout the night of Brahmā. But as day comes, the water gradually disappears.

paras tasmāt tu bhāvo 'nyo
'vyakto 'vyaktāt sanātanaḥ
yaḥ sa sarveṣu bhūteṣu
naśyatsu na vinaśyati

"Yet there is another unmanifest nature, which is eternal and is transcendental to this manifested and unmanifested matter. It is supreme and is never annihilated. When all in this world is annihilated, that part remains as it is." (Bg. 8.20)

We cannot calculate the extent of the material universe, but we have Vedic information that there are millions of universes within the entire creation and that beyond these material universes there is another sky, which is spiritual. There all the planets are eternal, and the lives of all the beings on them are eternal. In this verse the word *bhāvaḥ* means "nature," and here another nature is indicated. In this world also we have experience of two natures. The living entity is spirit, and as long as he is within matter, matter is moving, and as soon as the living entity, the spiritual spark, is out of the body, the body does not move. The spiritual nature is called Kṛṣṇa's superior nature, and the material is called the inferior. Beyond this material nature there is a superior nature, which is totally spiritual. It is not possible to understand this by experimental knowledge. We can see millions and millions of stars through a telescope, but we cannot approach them. We have to understand our incapabilities. If by experimental knowledge we cannot understand the material universe, what is the possibility of understanding God and His kingdom by these means? It is not possible. We have to understand by hearing the *Bhagavad-gītā*. We cannot understand who our father is by experimental knowledge; we have to hear the words of our mother and believe her. If we do not believe her, there is no way of knowing. Similarly, if we just stick to the Kṛṣṇa conscious method, all information about Kṛṣṇa and His kingdom will be revealed.

Paraḥ bhāvaḥ means "superior nature," and *vyaktaḥ* refers to what we see manifested. We can see that the material universe is manifested through the earth, sun, stars, and planets. And beyond this universe is another nature, an eternal nature. *Avyaktāt sanātanaḥ*. This material nature has a beginning and an end, but that spiritual nature is *sanātana*, eternal. It has neither beginning nor end. How is this possible? A cloud may pass over the sky and appear to cover a great portion of it, but actually the cloud is only a small speck covering an insignificant part of the whole sky. Because we are so small, if only a few hundred miles are covered by the cloud, to us it appears that the whole sky is covered. Similarly, this whole material universe is like a small, insignificant cloud in the vast spiritual sky. This material universe is encased by the *mahat-tattva*, matter. As a cloud has a beginning and an end, this material nature also has a beginning and an end. When the cloud disappears and the sky clears, we see everything as it is. Similarly, the body is like a cloud passing over the spirit soul. It stays for some time, gives some by-products, dwindles, and then vanishes. Any kind of material phenomenon that we observe is subject to the six transformations of material nature: it comes into being, grows, stays for a while, produces some by-products, dwindles, and then vanishes. Kṛṣṇa indicates that beyond this changing, cloud-like nature there is a spiritual nature, which is eternal. When this material nature is annihilated, that nature will remain.

In the Vedic literatures there is a good deal of information about the material and spiritual skies. In the Second Canto of *Śrīmad-Bhāgavatam* there are descriptions of the spiritual sky and its inhabitants. It is even said that there are spiritual airplanes in the spiritual sky and that the liberated entities there travel about on these planes like lightning. Everything that we find here can also be found there in reality. *Śrīmad-Bhāgavatam* states that here in the material sky everything is an imitation, or shadow, of that which exists in the spiritual sky. As in a cinema we simply see a facsimile of the real thing, so this material world is but a combination of matter modeled after the reality, just as a mannequin of a girl in a store window is modeled after a girl. Every sane man knows that the mannequin is an imitation. Śrīdhara Svāmī says that it is because the spiritual world is real that this material world, which is an imitation, *appears* to be real. We must understand the meaning of reality. Reality means existence which cannot be vanquished; reality means eternity.

nāsato vidyate bhāvo
nābhāvo vidyate sataḥ
ubhayor api dṛṣṭo 'ntas
tv anayos tattva-darśibhiḥ

"Those who are seers of the truth have concluded that of the nonexistent there is no endurance and of the existent there is no cessation. This seers have concluded by studying the nature of both." (Bg. 2.16)

Real pleasure is Kṛṣṇa, whereas material pleasure, which is temporary, is not actual. Those who can see things as they are do not take part in shadow pleasure. The real aim of human life is to attain to the spiritual sky, but as *Śrīmad-Bhāgavatam* points out, most people do not know about it. Human life is meant to understand reality and to be transferred into it. All Vedic literature instructs us not to remain in this darkness. The nature of this material world is darkness, but the spiritual world is full of light and yet is not illumined by fire or electricity. Kṛṣṇa states this in the Fifteenth Chapter of the *Bhagavad-gītā* (15.6):

na tad bhāsayate sūryo
na śaśāṅko na pāvakaḥ
yad gatvā na nivartante
tad dhāma paramaṁ mama

"That abode of Mine is not illumined by the sun or moon, nor by fire or electricity. Those who reach it never return to this material world."

The spiritual world is called unmanifested because one cannot perceive it with material senses.

avyakto 'kṣara ity uktas
tam āhuḥ paramāṁ gatim
yaṁ prāpya na nivartante
tad dhāma paramaṁ mama

"That which the Vedāntists describe as unmanifest and infallible, that which is known as the supreme destination, that place from which, having attained it, one never returns—that is My supreme abode." (Bg. 8.21) A great journey is indicated in this verse. We have to be able to penetrate outer space, traverse the material universe, penetrate its covering, and enter the spiritual sky. This is the supreme journey. There is no question of going a few thousand miles away from this planet and then returning. This sort of journey is not very heroic. We have to penetrate the whole material universe and enter the spiritual sky. This we can do not by spaceships but by Kṛṣṇa consciousness. One who is absorbed in Kṛṣṇa consciousness and who at the time of death thinks of Kṛṣṇa is at once transferred there. If we at all want to go to that spiritual sky and attain real, eternal, blissful life full of knowledge, we have to begin now to cultivate our *sac-cid-ānanda* body. It is said that Kṛṣṇa has a *sac-cid-ānanda* body—*īśvaraḥ paramaḥ kṛṣṇaḥ sac-cid-ānanda-vigrahaḥ*—and we also have a similar body of eternity, knowledge, and bliss. But ours is very small and is covered by the dress of this material body. If somehow or other we are able to give up this false dress, we can reach that spiritual kingdom. And once we can attain to that spiritual world, we will never have to come back (*yaṁ prāpya na nivartante*).

Everyone, then, should try to go to Kṛṣṇa's supreme abode. Kṛṣṇa Himself comes to call us, and He gives us literatures as guidebooks and sends His bona fide representatives to teach us. We should take advantage of this facility given to human beings. For one who reaches that supreme abode, penances, austerities, yogic meditations, and so on are no longer required, and for one who does not reach it, all penances and austerities are a useless waste of time. The human form of life is an opportunity to get this boon, and it is the duty of the state, parents, teachers, and guardians to elevate those who have acquired this human form of life to this perfection. Simply eating, sleeping, mating, and quarreling like cats and dogs is not civilization. We should properly utilize this human form of life and take advantage of this knowledge to prepare ourselves in Kṛṣṇa consciousness, so that twenty-four hours a day we will be absorbed in thoughts of Kṛṣṇa and at death at once transfer to that spiritual sky.

puruṣaḥ sa paraḥ pārtha
bhaktyā labhyas tv ananyayā
yasyāntaḥ-sthāni bhūtāni
yena sarvam idaṁ tatam

"The Supreme Personality of Godhead, who is greater than all, is attainable by unalloyed devotion. Although He is present in His abode, He is all-pervading, and everything is situated within Him." (Bg. 8.22) If we are at all interested in reaching that supreme abode, the process, as indicated here, is *bhakti*. *Bhakti* means devotional service, submission to the Supreme Lord. The root of the word *bhakti* is *bhaj*, which means "service." The definition of *bhakti* is given in the *Nārada-pañcarātra:*

sarvopādhi-vinirmuktaṁ
tat-paratvena nirmalam
hṛṣīkeṇa hṛṣīkeśa-
sevanaṁ bhaktir ucyate

"*Bhakti* means engaging all one's senses in the devotional service of the Supreme Personality of Godhead, the master of the senses. The result is that one is freed from all material designations and one's senses are purified." If one is determined to get out of all the designations that are attached to the pure spirit soul, and which arise due to the body and are always changed when the body is changed, one can attain to *bhakti.* To practice *bhakti* one must realize that he is pure spirit and not matter at all. Our real identity is not this body, which is simply a covering of the spirit; our real identity is *dāsa,* servant of Kṛṣṇa. When one is situated in his real identity and is rendering service to Kṛṣṇa, he is a *bhakta. Hṛṣīkeṇa hṛṣīkeśa-sevanam:* when our senses are free from material designations, we will utilize them in the service of the master of the senses, Hṛṣīkeśa, or Kṛṣṇa.

As Rūpa Gosvāmī points out, we have to serve Kṛṣṇa favorably. Generally we want to serve God for some material purpose or gain. Of course, one who goes to God for material gain is better than one who never goes, but we should be free from desire for material benefit. Our aim should be to understand Kṛṣṇa. Of course, Kṛṣṇa is unlimited, and so it is not possible to understand Him fully, but we have to accept what we *can* understand. Since we have to serve Kṛṣṇa favorably, for His pleasure, we need to understand what will please Him. How can we know this? From books like the *Bhagavad-gītā.* The *Bhagavad-gītā* is specifically presented for our understanding, and when we receive the right interpretation from the right person, we can know what will please Kṛṣṇa. Then we should serve Him favorably. Kṛṣṇa consciousness is a great science with immense literatures, and we should utilize them for the attainment of *bhakti.*

In the spiritual sky, the Supreme Lord is present as the Supreme Person, *puruṣaḥ paraḥ.* There are innumerable self-luminous planets there, and in each one an expansion of Kṛṣṇa resides. They are four-armed and have innumerable names. They are all persons—they are not impersonal. These *puruṣas,* or persons, can be approached by *bhakti,* not by challenge, philosophical speculation, or mental concoctions, nor by physical exercises, but by devotion without the deviations of fruitive activity.

What is the Supreme Person like? *Yasyāntaḥ-sthāni bhūtāni yena sarvam idaṁ tatam:* every living entity and everything is within Him, and yet He is without, all-pervading. How is that? He is just like the sun, which is situated in one place and yet is present all over by its rays. Although God is situated in His supreme abode, His energies are distributed everywhere. Nor is He different from His energies, inasmuch as the sun and the sunshine are nondifferent. Since Kṛṣṇa and His energies are nondifferent, we can see Kṛṣṇa everywhere if we are advanced in devotional service.

premāñjana-cchurita-bhakti-vilocanena
santaḥ sadaiva hṛdayeṣu vilokayanti
yaṁ śyāmasundaram acintya-guṇa-svarūpaṁ
govindam ādi-puruṣaṁ tam ahaṁ bhajāmi

"I worship the original Personality of Godhead, Govinda, whom the pure devotees whose eyes are smeared with the ointment of love of Godhead always see within their hearts." (*Brahma-saṁhitā* 5.38) Those who are filled with love of God see God constantly before them. It is not that we saw God last night and He is no longer present. No. For one who is Kṛṣṇa conscious, Kṛṣṇa is always present and can be perceived constantly. We simply have to develop the eyes to see Him.

Due to our material bondage, the covering of the material senses, we cannot understand what is spiritual. But this ignorance can be removed by the process of chanting Hare Kṛṣṇa. How is this? A sleeping man may be awakened by sound vibration. Although a sleeping man cannot see, feel, smell, or taste, the sense of hearing is so prominent that he can be awakened by sound. Similarly, the spirit soul, although now overpowered by the sleep of material contact, can be revived by the transcendental sound vibration of Hare Kṛṣṇa, Hare Kṛṣṇa, Kṛṣṇa Kṛṣṇa, Hare Hare/ Hare Rāma, Hare Rāma, Rāma Rāma, Hare Hare. Hare Kṛṣṇa is simply an address to the Supreme Lord and His energy. *Hare* means the Lord's energy, and *kṛṣṇa* is a name of the Supreme Lord, so when we chant Hare Kṛṣṇa we are saying, "O energy of the Lord, O Lord, please accept me as Your servant." We do not pray for anything else. Lord Caitanya Mahāprabhu Himself prayed,

ayi nanda-tanuja kiṅkaraṁ
patitaṁ māṁ viṣame bhavāmbudhau
kṛpayā tava pāda-paṅkaja-
sthita-dhūlī-sadṛśaṁ vicintaya

"O son of Mahārāja Nanda, I am Your eternal servitor, and although I am so, somehow or other I have fallen into the ocean of birth and death. Please, therefore, pick me up from this ocean of death and fix me as one of the atoms at Your lotus feet." (*Śikṣāṣṭaka* 5) The only hope for a man fallen into the middle of the ocean is that someone will come and pick him up. If someone comes and lifts him but a few feet out of the water, he is immediately relieved. Similarly, if we are lifted from the ocean of birth and death by the process of Kṛṣṇa consciousness, we are immediately relieved.

Although we cannot perceive the transcendental nature of the Supreme Lord—His name, form, qualities, and activities—if we establish ourselves in Kṛṣṇa consciousness, gradually God will reveal Himself before us. We cannot see God by our own endeavor, but if we qualify ourselves, God will reveal Himself, and then we will see. No one can order God to come before him and dance, but we can work in such a way that Kṛṣṇa will be pleased to reveal Himself to us.

Kṛṣṇa gives us information about Himself in the *Bhagavad-gītā,* and there is no question of doubting it; we just have to feel it, to understand it. There is no preliminary qualification necessary for understanding the *Bhagavad-gītā,* because it is spoken from the absolute platform. The simple process of chanting the names of Kṛṣṇa will reveal what one is, what God is, what the material and spiritual universes are, why we are conditioned, how we can get out of that conditioning—everything will be revealed, step by step. Actually, the process of belief and revelation is not foreign to us. Every day we place our faith in something that we have confidence will be revealed later. We may purchase a ticket to go to India, and on the basis of the ticket we have faith that we will be transported there. Why should we pay money for a ticket? We do not just give the money to anyone. The company is authorized and the airline is authorized, so faith is created. Without faith we cannot take one step forward in the ordinary course of our life. Faith we must have, but it must be faith in that which is authorized. It is not that we have blind faith, but that we accept something that is recognized. The *Bhagavad-gītā* is recognized and accepted as scripture by all classes of men in India, and as far as outside India is concerned, many scholars, theologians, and philosophers accept the *Bhagavad-gītā* as a great, authoritative work. There is no question that the *Bhagavad-gītā* is authoritative. Even Professor Albert Einstein, such a great scientist, read the *Bhagavad-gītā* regularly.

From the *Bhagavad-gītā* we have to accept that there is a spiritual universe which is the kingdom of God. If somehow we were transported to a country where we were informed that we would no longer have to undergo birth, old age, disease, and death, would we not be happy? If we heard of such a place, surely we would try as hard as possible to go there. No one wants to grow old; no one wants to die. Indeed, a place free of such sufferings would be our heart's desire. Why do we want this? Because we have the right, the prerogative, to want it. We are eternal, blissful, and full of knowledge, but having been covered by this material entanglement, we have forgotten ourselves. Therefore the *Bhagavad-gītā* gives us the advantage of being able to revive our original status.

The Śaṅkarites and Buddhists claim that the world beyond is void, but the *Bhagavad-gītā* does not disappoint us like this. The philosophy of voidness has simply created atheists. We are spiritual beings, and we want enjoyment, but as soon as we think our future is void, we will become inclined to enjoy this material life. In this way, the impersonalists discuss the philosophy of voidism while trying as much as possible to enjoy this material life. One may enjoy speculation in this way, but there is no spiritual benefit.

brahma-bhūtaḥ prasannātmā
na śocati na kāṅkṣati
samaḥ sarveṣu bhūteṣu
mad-bhaktiṁ labhate parām

"One who is thus transcendentally situated at once realizes the Supreme Brahman and becomes fully joyful. He never laments or desires to have anything; he is equally disposed to every living entity. In that state he attains pure devotional service unto Me." (Bg. 18.54)

He who has progressed in devotional life and who is relishing service to Kṛṣṇa will automatically become detached from material enjoyment. The symptom of one absorbed in *bhakti* is that he is fully satisfied with Kṛṣṇa.

Five

Associating with Kṛṣṇa

If one gets something superior, he naturally gives up all inferior things. We want enjoyment, but impersonalism and voidism have created such an atmosphere that we have become addicted to material enjoyment. There must be enjoyment in connection with the Supreme Person, whom we can see face to face. In the spiritual sky we are able to speak personally with God, play with Him, eat with Him, etc. All of this can be attained by *bhakti*—transcendental loving service to the Lord. However, this service must be without adulteration, that is to say, we must love God without expecting material remuneration. Loving God to become one with Him is also a form of adulteration.

One of the major differences between the spiritual sky and the material sky is that in the spiritual sky the leader of the spiritual planets has no rival. In all cases, the predominating personality in the spiritual planets is a plenary expansion of Śrī Kṛṣṇa. The Supreme Lord and His multifarious manifestations preside over all the Vaikuṇṭha planets. On earth there is rivalry for the position of president or prime minister, but in the spiritual sky everyone acknowledges the Supreme Personality of Godhead to be supreme. Those who do not acknowledge Him and attempt to become His rivals are placed into the material universe, which is just like a prison house. In every city there is a prison, which forms a very insignificant part of the whole city. Similarly, within the spiritual sky is a prison for the conditioned souls, and that prison is the material universe. It forms an insignificant part of the spiritual sky, but it is not outside the spiritual sky, just as a prison is not outside the city.

The inhabitants of the Vaikuṇṭha planets in the spiritual sky are all liberated souls. In *Śrīmad-Bhāgavatam* we are informed that their bodily features are exactly like God's. On these planets God is manifested with four arms. Like the Supreme Lord, the inhabitants of these planets, also have four arms, and it is said that one cannot distinguish between them and the Supreme Person. In the spiritual world there are five kinds of liberation. *Sāyujya-mukti* is a form of liberation in which one merges into the impersonal existence of the Supreme Lord, called Brahman. Another form of liberation is *sārūpya-mukti,* by which one receives features exactly like God's. Another is *sālokya-mukti,* by which one can live on the same planet as God. By *sārṣṭi-mukti* one can have opulences similar to the Supreme Lord's. And *sāmīpya-mukti* enables one to remain always with God as one of His associates, just like Arjuna, who is always with Kṛṣṇa as His friend. One can have any of these five forms of liberation, but of the five, merging with the impersonal aspect (*sāyujya-mukti)* is not accepted by Vaiṣṇavas, or devotees. A Vaiṣṇava wishes to worship God as He is and retain his separate individuality to serve Him, whereas the impersonal Māyāvādī philosopher wishes to lose his individuality and merge into the existence of the Supreme. This merging is recommended neither by Śrī Kṛṣṇa in the *Bhagavad-gītā* nor by the disciplic succession of Vaiṣṇava philosophers. Lord Caitanya Mahāprabhu wrote on this subject in His *Śikṣāṣṭaka* (4):

na dhanaṁ na janaṁ na sundarīṁ
kavitāṁ vā jagad-īśa kāmaye

mama janmani janmanīśvare
bhavatād bhaktir ahaitukī tvayi

"O almighty Lord, I have no desire to accumulate wealth, nor do I desire beautiful women, nor do I want any number of followers. I only want Your causeless devotional service in my life, birth after birth." Here Lord Caitanya Mahāprabhu refers to "birth after birth." When there is birth after birth, there is no liberation. In liberation one either attains to the spiritual planets or merges into the existence of the Supreme—in either case, there is no question of rebirth into the material world. But Caitanya Mahāprabhu doesn't care whether He is liberated or not: His only concern is to be engaged in Kṛṣṇa consciousness, to serve the Supreme Lord. The devotee doesn't care where he is, nor does he care whether he is born in the animal society, human society, demigod society, or whatever. He only prays to God that he not forget Him and that he always be able to engage in His transcendental service. This kind of prayer is a symptom of pure devotion. Of course, wherever he is, a devotee remains in the spiritual kingdom, even while in this material body. But he does not demand anything from God for his own personal elevation or comfort.

Śrī Kṛṣṇa indicates that while He can be easily reached by one who is devoted to Him, there is an element of risk involved for the *yogīs* who practice other methods of *yoga*. For them, He has given directions in the *Bhagavad-gītā* (8.23) regarding the proper time to leave the gross body.

yatra kāle tv anāvṛttim
āvṛttiṁ caiva yoginaḥ
prayātā yānti taṁ kālaṁ
vakṣyāmi bharatarṣabha

"O best of the Bhāratas, I shall now explain to you the different times at which, passing away from this world, one does or does not come back." Here Kṛṣṇa indicates that if one is able to leave his body at a particular time, he can become liberated, never to return to the material world. On the other hand, He indicates that if one dies at another time, he has to return. There is this element of chance. But there is no question of chance for a devotee always in Kṛṣṇa consciousness, for he is guaranteed entrance into the abode of Kṛṣṇa by dint of his devotion to the Lord.

agnir jyotir ahaḥ śuklaḥ
ṣaṇ-māsā uttarāyaṇam
tatra prayātā gacchanti
brahma brahma-vido janāḥ

"Those who know the Supreme Brahman attain that Supreme by passing away from the world during the influence of the fiery god, in the light, at an auspicious moment of the day, during the fortnight of the waxing moon, or during the six months when the sun travels in the north." (Bg. 8.24) The sun spends six months in a northern orbit and six months in a southern orbit. In *Śrīmad-Bhāgavatam* we have information that as the planets are moving, so also is the sun moving. If one who knows Brahman dies when the sun is in its northern course, he attains liberation.

dhūmo rātris tathā kṛṣṇaḥ
ṣaṇ-māsā dakṣiṇāyanam
tatra cāndramasaṁ jyotir
yogī prāpya nivartate

śukla-kṛṣṇe gatī hy ete
jagataḥ śāśvate mate

ekayā yāty anāvṛttim
anyayāvartate punaḥ

"The mystic who passes away from this world during the smoke, the night, the fortnight of the waning moon, or the six months when the sun passes to the south reaches the moon planet but again comes back. According to Vedic opinion, there are two ways of passing from this world—one in light and one in darkness. When one passes in light, he does not come back; but when one passes in darkness, he returns." (Bg. 8.25–26)

This is all by chance. We do not know when we are going to die, for we may die accidentally at any time. But for one who is a *bhakti-yogī*, who is established in Kṛṣṇa consciousness, there is no question of chance. He is always sure.

naite sṛtī pārtha jānan
yogī muhyati kaścana
tasmāt sarveṣu kāleṣu
yoga-yukto bhavārjuna

"The devotees know these two paths, O Arjuna, and are thus never bewildered. Therefore, be always fixed in devotion." (Bg. 8.27)

It has already been ascertained that at the time of death one who thinks of Kṛṣṇa is immediately transferred to the abode of Kṛṣṇa.

anta-kāle ca mām eva
smaran muktvā kalevaram
yaḥ prayāti sa mad-bhāvaṁ
yāti nāsty atra saṁśayaḥ

abhyāsa-yoga-yuktena
cetasā nānya-gāminā

paramaṁ puruṣaṁ divyaṁ
yāti pārthānucintayan

"And whoever, at the time of death, quits his body remembering Me alone at once attains My nature. Of this there is no doubt. He who meditates on Me as the Supreme Personality of Godhead, his mind constantly engaged in remembering Me, undeviated from the path, he, O Pārtha, is sure to reach Me." (Bg. 8.5, 8.8) Such meditation on Kṛṣṇa may seem very difficult, but it is not. If one practices Kṛṣṇa consciousness by chanting the *mahā-mantra*, Hare Kṛṣṇa, Hare Kṛṣṇa, Kṛṣṇa Kṛṣṇa, Hare Hare/ Hare Rāma, Hare Rāma, Rāma Rāma, Hare Hare, he will be quickly helped. Kṛṣṇa and His name are nondifferent, and Kṛṣṇa and His transcendental abode are also nondifferent. By sound vibration we can associate with Kṛṣṇa. If, for instance, we chant Hare Kṛṣṇa on the street, we will see that Kṛṣṇa is going with us, just as when we look up and see the moon overhead we perceive that it is also going with us. If Kṛṣṇa's inferior energy may appear to go with us, is it not possible for Kṛṣṇa Himself to be with us when we are chanting His names? He will keep us company, but we have to qualify to be in His company. If, however, we are always merged in the thought of Kṛṣṇa, we should rest assured that Kṛṣṇa is always with us. Lord Caitanya Mahāprabhu prays,

nāmnām akāri bahudhā nija-sarva-śaktis
tatrārpitā niyamitaḥ smaraṇe na kālaḥ
etādṛśī tava kṛpā bhagavan mamāpi
durdaivam īdṛśam ihājani nānurāgaḥ

"O my Lord, Your holy name alone can render all benediction to living beings, and thus You have hundreds and millions of names, like Kṛṣṇa and Govinda. In these transcendental names You have invested all Your transcendental energies, and there are no hard and fast rules for chanting these names. O my Lord, out of kindness You enable us to easily approach You by chanting Your holy names, but I am so unfortunate that I have no attraction for them." (*Śikṣāṣṭaka* 2)

Merely by chanting the Hare Kṛṣṇa *mahā-mantra* we can have all the advantages of personal association with Kṛṣṇa. Lord Caitanya Mahāprabhu, who is considered not only a realized soul but an incarnation of Kṛṣṇa Himself, has pointed out that in this Age of Kali, although people have no real facilities for self-realization, Kṛṣṇa is so kind that He has descended in the form of transcendental sound, His holy names. Chanting these names is the *yuga-dharma,* or way of realization for this age. No special qualification is necessary for this method; we need not even know Sanskrit. The Hare Kṛṣṇa *mantra* is so potent that anyone can immediately begin chanting it, without any knowledge of Sanskrit whatsoever.

vedeṣu yajñeṣu tapaḥsu caiva
dāneṣu yat puṇya-phalaṁ pradiṣṭam
atyeti tat sarvam idaṁ viditvā
yogī paraṁ sthānam upaiti cādyam

"A person who accepts the path of devotional service is not bereft of the results derived from studying the *Vedas,* performing sacrifices, undergoing austerities, giving charity or pursuing philosophical and fruitive activities. Simply by performing devotional service, he attains all these, and at the end he reaches the supreme abode." (Bg. 8.28) Here Kṛṣṇa says that the purpose of all Vedic instructions is to achieve the ultimate goal of life—to go back to Godhead. All scriptures from all countries aim at this goal. This has also been the message of all religious reformers or *ācāryas.* In the West, for example, Lord Jesus Christ spread this same message. So did

Lord Buddha and Muhammad. None of them advised us to try to make our permanent settlement here in this material world. There may be small differences according to country, time, and circumstance, and according to scriptural injunction, but the main principle that we are meant not for this material world but for the spiritual world is accepted by all genuine transcendentalists. All indications for the satisfaction of our soul's innermost desires point to those worlds of Kṛṣṇa beyond birth and death.

The Author

His Divine Grace A. C. Bhaktivedanta Swami Prabhupāda appeared in this world in 1896 in Calcutta, India. He first met his spiritual master, Śrīla Bhaktisiddhānta Sarasvatī Gosvāmī, in Calcutta in 1922. Bhaktisiddhānta Sarasvatī, a prominent religious scholar and the founder of sixty-four Gauḍīya Maṭhas (Vedic institutes), liked this educated young man and convinced him to dedicate his life to teaching Vedic knowledge. Śrīla Prabhupāda became his student and, in 1933, his formally initiated disciple.

At their first meeting, in 1922, Śrīla Bhaktisiddhānta Sarasvatī requested Śrīla Prabhupāda to broadcast Vedic knowledge in English. In the years that followed, Śrīla Prabhupāda wrote a commentary on the *Bhagavad-gītā*, assisted the Gauḍīya Maṭha in its work, and, in 1944, started *Back to Godhead*, an English fortnightly magazine. Single-handedly, Śrīla Prabhupāda edited it, typed the manuscripts, checked the galley proofs, and even distributed the individual copies. The magazine is now being continued by his followers.

In 1950 Śrīla Prabhupāda retired from married life, adopting the *vānaprastha* (retired) order to devote more time to his studies and writing. He traveled to the holy city of Vṛndāvana, where he lived in humble circumstances in the historic temple of Rādhā-Dāmodara. There he engaged for several years in deep study and writing. He accepted the renounced order of life (*sannyāsa*) in 1959. At Rādhā-Dāmodara, Śrīla Prabhupāda began work on his life's masterpiece: a multivolume commentated translation of the eighteen-thousand-verse *Śrīmad-Bhāgavatam* (*Bhāgavata Purāṇa*). He also wrote *Easy Journey to Other Planets.*

After publishing three volumes of the *Bhāgavatam*, Śrīla Prabhupāda came to the United States, in September 1965, to fulfill the mission of his spiritual master. Subsequently, His Divine Grace wrote more than fifty volumes of authoritative commentated translations and summary studies of the philosophical and religious classics of India.

When he first arrived by freighter in New York City, Śrīla Prabhupāda was practically penniless. Only after almost a year of great difficulty did he establish the International Society for Krishna Consciousness, in July of 1966. Before he passed away on November 14, 1977, he had guided the Society and seen it grow to a worldwide confederation of more than one hundred *āśramas*, schools, temples, institutes, and farm communities.

In 1972 His Divine Grace introduced the Vedic system of primary and secondary education in the West by founding the *gurukula* school in Dallas, Texas. Since then his disciples have established similar schools throughout the United States and the rest of the world.

Śrīla Prabhupāda also inspired the construction of several large international cultural centers in India. At Śrīdhāma Māyāpur, in West Bengal, devotees are building a spiritual city centered on a magnificent temple—an ambitious project for which construction will extend over many years to come. In Vṛndāvana are the Kṛṣṇa-Balarāma Temple and International Guesthouse, *gurukula* school, and Śrīla Prabhupāda Memorial and Museum. There are also major temples and cultural centers in Mumbai, New Delhi, Ahmedabad, Siliguri, and Ujjain. Other centers are planned in many important locations on the Indian subcontinent.

Śrīla Prabhupāda's most significant contribution, however, is his books. Highly respected by scholars for their authority, depth, and clarity, they are used as textbooks in numerous college courses. His writings have been translated into over fifty languages. The Bhaktivedanta Book Trust, established in 1972 to publish the works of His Divine Grace, has thus become the world's largest publisher of books in the field of Indian religion and philosophy.

In just twelve years, despite his advanced age, Śrīla Prabhupāda circled the globe fourteen times on lecture tours that took him to six continents. In spite of such a vigorous schedule, Śrīla Prabhupāda continued to write prolifically. His writings constitute a veritable library of Vedic philosophy, religion, literature, and culture.

The International Society for Krishna Consciousness
Founder-Ācārya: His Divine Grace A.C. Bhaktivedanta Swami Prabhupāda

CENTERS AROUND THE WORLD

(Partial List)

CANADA

Brampton-Mississauga, Ontario — Unit 20, 1030 Kamato Dr., L4W 4B6/Tel. (416) 840-6587 or (905) 826-1290/ iskconbrampton@gmail.com

Calgary, Alberta — 313 Fourth St. N.E., T2E 3S3/ Tel. (403) 265-3302/ Fax: (403) 547-0795/vamanstones@shaw.ca

Edmonton, Alberta — 9353 35th Ave. NW, T6E 5R5/ Tel. (780) 439-9999/ harekrishna.edmonton@gmail.com

Montreal, Quebec — 1626 Pie IX Blvd., H1V 2C5/ Tel. & fax: (514) 521-1301/ iskconmontreal@gmail.com

♦ **Ottawa, Ontario** — 212 Somerset St. E., K1N 6V4/ Tel. (613) 565-6544/ Fax: (613) 565-2575/iskconottawa@sympatico.ca

Regina, Saskatchewan — 1279 Retallack St., S4T 2H8/ Tel. (306) 525-0002 or -6461/jagadishadas@yahoo.com

Toronto, Ontario — 243 Avenue Rd., M5R 2J6/ Tel. (416) 922-5415/ Fax: (416) 922-1021/ toronto@iskcon.net

Vancouver, B.C. — 5462 S.E. Marine Dr., Burnaby V5J 3G8/ Tel. (604) 433-9728/ Fax: (604) 648-8715/akrura@krishna.com; Govinda's Bookstore & Cafe/ Tel. (604) 433-7100 or 1-888-433-8722

RURAL COMMUNITY

Ashcroft, B.C. — Saranagati Dhama, Venables Valley (mail: P.O. Box 99, VOK 1A0)/ Tel. (250) 457-7438/Fax: (250) 453-9306/ iskconsaranagati@hotmail.com

U.S.A.

Atlanta, Georgia — 1287 South Ponce de Leon Ave. N.E., 30306/ Tel. & fax: (404) 377-8680/ admin@atlantaharekrishnas.com

Austin, Texas — 10700 Jonwood Way, 78753/ Tel. (512) 835-2121/ Fax: (512) 835-8479/ sda@backtohome.com

Baltimore, Maryland —200 Bloomsbury Ave., Catonsville, 21228/ Tel. (410) 719-1776/ Fax: (410) 799-0642/ info@baltimorekrishna.com

Berkeley, California — 2334 Stuart St., 94705/ Tel. (510) 649-8619/ Fax: (510) 665-9366/ rajan416@yahoo.com

Boise, Idaho — 1615 Martha St., 83706/ Tel. (208) 344-4274/ boise_temple@yahoo.com

Boston, Massachusetts — 72 Commonwealth Ave., 02116/ Tel. (617) 247-8611/ Fax: (617) 909-5181/ darukrishna@iskconboston.org

Chicago, Illinois — 1716 W. Lunt Ave., 60626/ Tel. (773) 973-0900/ Fax: (773) 973-0526/ chicagoiskcon@yahoo.com

Columbus, Ohio — 379 W. Eighth Ave., 43201/ Tel. (614) 421-1661/ Fax: (614) 294-0545/ rmanjari@sbcglobal.net

♦ **Dallas, Texas** — 5430 Gurley Ave., 75223/ Tel. (214) 827-6330/ Fax: (214) 823-7264/ txkrishnas@aol.com; restaurant: vegetariantaste@aol.com

♦ **Denver, Colorado** — 1400 Cherry St., 80220/ Tel. (303) 333-5461/ Fax: (303) 321-9052/ info@krishnadenver.com

Detroit, Michigan — 383 Lenox Ave., 48215/ Tel. (313) 824-6000/ gaurangi108@hotmail.com

Gainesville, Florida — 214 N.W. 14th St., 32603/ Tel. (352) 336-4183/ Fax: (352) 379-2927/ kalakantha.acbsp@pamho.net

Hartford, Connecticut — 1683 Main St., E. Hartford 06108/ Tel. & fax: (860) 289-7252/ pyari@sbcglobal.net

♦ **Honolulu, Hawaii** — 51 Coelho Way, 96817/ Tel. (808) 595-4913/ rama108@bigfoot.com

Houston, Texas — 1320 W. 34th St., 77018/ Tel. (713) 686-4482/ Fax: (713) 956-9968/ management@iskconhouston.org

Kansas City, Missouri — 5201 Paseo Blvd./ Tel. (816) 924-5619/ Fax: (816) 924-5640/ rvc@rvc.edu

Laguna Beach, California — 285 Legion St., 92651/ Tel. (949) 494-7029/ info@lagunatemple.com

Las Vegas, Nevada — Govinda's Center of Vedic India, 6380 S. Eastern Ave., Suite 8, 89120/ Tel. (702) 434-8332/ info@govindascenter.com

♦ **Los Angeles, California** — 3764 Watseka Ave., 90034/ Tel. (310) 836-2676/ Fax: (310) 839-2715/ membership@harekrishnala.com

♦ **Miami, Florida** — 3220 Virginia St., 33133 (mail: 3109 Grand Ave. #491, Coconut Grove, FL 33133)/ Tel. (305) 442-7218/ devotionalservice@iskcon-miami.org

New Orleans, Louisiana — 2936 Esplanade Ave., 70119/ Tel. (504) 304-0032 (office) or (504) 638-3244/ iskcon.new.orleans@pamho.net

♦ **New York, New York** — 305 Schermerhorn St., Brooklyn 11217/ Tel. (718) 855-6714/ Fax: (718) 875-6127/ ramabhadra@aol.com

New York, New York — 26 Second Ave., 10003/ Tel. (212) 253-6182/ krishnanyc@gmail.com

Orlando, Florida — 2651 Rouse Rd., 32817/ Tel. (407) 257-3865

Philadelphia, Pennsylvania — 41 West Allens Lane, 19119/ Tel. (215) 247-4600/ Fax: (215) 247-8702/ savecows@aol.com

♦ **Philadelphia, Pennsylvania** — 1408 South St., 19146/ Tel. (215) 985-9303/ savecows@aol.com

Phoenix, Arizona — 100 S. Weber Dr., Chandler, 85226/ Tel. (480) 705-4900/ Fax: (480) 705-4901/ svgd108@yahoo.com

Portland, Oregon — 2095 NW Alocleck Dr., Suites 1107 & 1109, Hillsboro 97124/ Tel. (503) 439-9117/ info@iskconportland.com

St. Augustine, Florida — 3001 First St., 32084/ Tel. & fax: (904) 819-0221/ vasudeva108@gmail.com

♦ **St. Louis, Missouri** — 3926 Lindell Blvd., 63108/ Tel. (314) 535-8085 or 534-1708/ Fax: (314) 535-0672/ rpsdas@gmail.com

San Antonio, Texas — 6772 Oxford Trace, 78240/ Tel. (210) 401-6576/ aadasa@gmail.com

♦ **San Diego, California** — 1030 Grand Ave., Pacific Beach 92109/ Tel. (310) 895-0104/ Fax: (858) 483-0941/ krishna.sandiego@gmail.com

San Jose, California — 951 S. Bascom Ave., 95128/ Tel. (408) 293-4959/ iskconsanjose@yahoo.com

Seattle, Washington — 1420 228th Ave. S.E., Sammamish 98075/ Tel. (425) 246-8436/ Fax: (425) 868-8928/ info@vedicculturalcenter.org

♦ **Spanish Fork, Utah** — Krishna Temple Project & KHQN Radio, 8628 S. State Rd., 84660/ Tel. (801) 798-3559/ Fax: (810) 798-9121/ carudas@earthlink.net

Tallahassee, Florida — 1323 Nylic St., 32304/ Tel. & fax: (850) 224-3803/ darudb@hotmail.com

Towaco, New Jersey — 100 Jacksonville Rd. (mail: P.O. Box 109), 07082/ Tel. & fax: (973) 299-0970/ newjersey@iskcon.net

♦ **Tucson, Arizona** — 711 E. Blacklidge Dr., 85719/ Tel. (520) 792-0630/ Fax: (520) 791-0906/ tucphx@cs.com

Washington, D.C. — 10310 Oaklyn Dr., Potomac, Maryland 20854/ Tel. (301) 299-2100/ Fax: (301) 299-5025/ ad@pamho.net

RURAL COMMUNITIES

♦ **Alachua, Florida (New Raman Reti)** — 17306 N.W. 112th Blvd., 32615 (mail: P.O. Box 819, 32616)/ Tel. (386) 462-2017/ Fax: (386) 462-2641/ alachuatemple@gmail.com

Carriere, Mississippi (New Talavan) — 31492 Anner Road, 39426/ Tel. (601) 749-9460 or 799-1354/ Fax: (601) 799-2924/ talavan@hughes.net

Gurabo, Puerto Rico (New Govardhana Hill) — Carr. 181, Km. 16.3, Bo. Santa Rita, Gurabo (mail: HC-01, Box 8440, Gurabo, PR 00778)/ Tel. (787) 367-3530 or (787) 737-1722/ manonath@

♦ Temples with restaurants or dining

gmail.com
Hillsborough, North Carolina (New Goloka) — 1032 Dimmocks Mill Rd., 27278/ Tel. (919) 732-6492/ bkgoswami@earthlink.net
Moundsville, West Virginia (New Vrindaban) — R.D. No. 1, Box 319, Hare Krishna Ridge, 26041/ Tel. (304) 843-1600; Visitors, (304) 845-5905/ Fax: (304) 845-0023/ mail@newvrindaban.com
Mulberry, Tennessee (Murari-sevaka) — 532 Murari Lane, 37359 (mail: P.O. Box 108, Lynchburg, TN 37352)/ Tel. (931) 227-6156/ Tel. & fax: (931) 759-6888/ murari_sevaka@yahoo.com
Port Royal, Pennsylvania (Gita Nagari) — 534 Gita Nagari Rd./ Tel. (717) 527-4101/ kaulinidasi@hotmail.com
Sandy Ridge, North Carolina — Prabhupada Village, 1283 Prabhupada Rd., 27046/ Tel. (336) 593-9888/ madanmohanmohinni@yahoo.com

ADDITIONAL RESTAURANTS

Hato Rey, Puerto Rico — Tamal Krishna's Veggie Garden, 131 Eleanor Roosevelt, 00918/ Tel. (787) 754-6959/ Fax: (787) 756-7769/ tkveggiegarden@aol.com
Seattle, Washington — My Sweet Lord, 5521 University Way, 98105/ Tel. (425) 643-4664

UNITED KINGDOM AND IRELAND

Belfast, Northern Ireland — Brooklands, 140 Upper Dunmurray Lane, BT17 OHE/ Tel. +44 (28) 9062 0530
Birmingham, England — 84 Stanmore Rd., Edgbaston B16 9TB/ Tel. +44 (121) 420 4999/ birmingham@iskcon.org.uk
Cardiff, Wales — The Soul Centre, 116 Cowbridge Rd., East Canton CF11 9DX/ Tel. +44 (29) 2039 0391/ the.soul.centre@pamho.net
Coventry, England — Kingfield Rd., Coventry (mail: 19 Gloucester St., Coventry CV1 3BZ)/ Tel. +44 (24) 7655 2822 or 5420/ haridas.kds@pamho.net
• **Dublin, Ireland** — 83 Middle Abbey St., Dublin 1/ Tel. +353 (1) 661 5095/ dublin@krishna.ie; Govinda's: info@govindas.ie
Lesmahagow, Scotland — Karuna Bhavan, Bankhouse Rd., Lesmahagow, Lanarkshire, ML11 0ES/ Tel. +44 (1555) 894790/ Fax: +44 (1555) 894526/ karunabhavan@aol.com
Leicester, England — 21 Thoresby St., North Evington, LE5 4GU/ Tel. +44 (116) 276 2587/ pradyumna.jas@pamho.net
• **London, England (city)** — 10 Soho St., W1D 3DL/ Tel. +44 (20) 7437-3662; residential /pujaris, 7439-3606; shop, 7287-0269; Govinda's Restaurant, 7437-4928/ Fax: +44 (20) 7439-1127/ london@pamho.net
• **London, England (country)** — Bhaktivedanta Manor, Dharam Marg, Hilfield Lane, Watford, Herts, WD25 8EZ/ Tel. +44 (1923) 851000/ Fax: +44 (1923) 851006/ info@krishnatemple.com; Guesthouse: bmguesthouse@krishna.com
London, England (south) — 42 Enmore Road, South Norwood, SE25 5NG/ Tel. +44 7988857530/ krishnaprema89@hotmail.com
London, England (Kings Cross) — 102 Caledonain Rd., Kings Cross, Islington, N1 9DN/ Tel. +44 (20) 7168 5732/ foodforalluk@aol.com
Manchester, England — 20 Mayfield Rd., Whalley Range, M16 8FT/ Tel. +44 (161) 226 4416/ contact@iskconmanchester.com
Newcastle-upon-Tyne, England — 304 Westgate Rd., NE4 6AR/ Tel. +44 (191) 272 1911
• **Swansea, Wales** — 8 Craddock St., SA1 3EN/ Tel. +44 (1792) 468469/ iskcon.swansea@pamho.net (restaurant: govindas@hotmail.com)

RURAL COMMUNITIES

Upper Lough Erne, Northern Ireland — Govindadwipa Dhama, Inisrath Island, Derrylin, Co. Fermanagh, BT92 9GN/ Tel. +44 (28) 6772 1512/ govindadwipa@pamho.net
London, England — (contact Bhaktivedanta Manor) Programs are held regularly in more than forty other cities in the UK. For information, contact ISKCON Reader Services, P.O. Box 730, Watford WD25 8EZ, UK; www.iskcon.org.uk

ADDITIONAL RESTAURANTS

Dublin, Ireland — Govinda's, 4 Aungier St., Dublin 2/ Tel. +353 (1) 475 0309/ Fax: +353 (1) 478 6204/ info@govindas.ie
Dublin, Ireland — Govinda's, 18 Merrion Row, Dublin 2/ Tel. +353 (1) 661 5095/ praghosa.sdg@pamho.net

AUSTRALASIA

AUSTRALIA

Adelaide — 25 Le Hunte St. (mail: P.O. Box 114, Kilburn, SA 5084)/ Tel. & fax: +61 (8) 8359-5120/ iskconsa@tpg.com.au
Brisbane — 95 Bank Rd., Graceville (mail: P.O. Box 83, Indooroopilly), QLD 4068/ Tel. +61 (7) 3379-5455/ Fax: +61 (7) 3379-5880/ brisbane@iskcon.org.au
Canberra — 1 Quick St., Ainslie, ACT 2602 (mail: P.O. Box 1411, Canberra, ACT 2601)/ Tel. & fax: +61 (2) 6262-6208/ iskcon@harekrishnacanberra.com
Melbourne — 197 Danks St. (mail: P.O. Box 125), Albert Park, VIC 3206/ Tel. +61 (3) 9699-5122/ Fax: +61 (3) 9690-4093/ melbourne@pamho.net
Newcastle — 28 Bull St., Mayfield, NSW 2304/ Tel. +61 (2) 4967-7000/ iskcon_newcastle@yahoo.com.au
Perth — 155–159 Canning Rd., Kalamunda (mail: P.O. Box 201 Kalamunda 6076)/ Tel. +61 (8) 6293-1519/ perth@pamho.net
Sydney — 180 Falcon St., North Sydney, NSW 2060 (mail: P.O. Box 459, Cammeray, NSW 2062)/ Tel. +61 (2) 9959-4558/ Fax: +61 (2) 9957-1893/ admin@iskcon.com.au
Sydney — Govinda's Yoga & Meditation Centre, 112 Darlinghurst Rd., Darlinghurst NSW 2010 (mail: P.O. Box 174, Kings Cross 1340)/ Tel. +61 (2) 9380-5162/ Fax: +61 (2) 9360-1736/ sita@govindas.com.au

RURAL COMMUNITIES

Bambra, VIC (New Nandagram) — 50 Seaches Outlet, off 1265 Winchelsea Deans Marsh Rd., Bambra VIC 3241/ Tel. +61 (3) 5288-7383
Cessnock, NSW (New Gokula) — Lewis Lane (Off Mount View Road, Millfield, near Cessnock [mail: P.O. Box 399, Cessnock, NSW 2325])/ Tel. +61 (2) 4998-1800/ Fax: (Sydney temple)/ iskconfarm@mac.com
Murwillumbah, NSW (New Govardhana) — Tyalgum Rd., Eungella (mail: P.O. Box 687), NSW 2484/ Tel. +61 (2) 6672-6579/ Fax: +61 (2) 6672-5498/ ajita@in.com.au

RESTAURANTS

Brisbane — Govinda's, 99 Elizabeth St., 1st Floor, QLD 4000/ Tel. +61 (7) 3210-0255
Brisbane — Krishna's Cafe, 1st Floor, 82 Vulture St., W. End, QLD 4000/ brisbane@pamho.net
Burleigh Heads — Govindas, 20 James St., Burleigh Heads, QLD 4220/ Tel. +61 (7) 5607-0782/ ajita@in.com.au
Cairns — Gaura Nitai's, 55 Spence St., Cairns, QLD/ Tel. +61 (7) 4031-2255 or (425) 725 901/ Fax: +61 (7) 4031 2256/ gauranitais@in.com.au
Maroochydore — Govinda's Vegetarian Cafe, 2/7 First Ave., QLD 4558/ Tel. +61 (7) 5451-0299
Melbourne — Crossways, 1st Floor, 123 Swanston St., VIC 3000/ Tel. +61 (3) 9650-2939
Melbourne — Gopal's, 139 Swanston St., VIC 3000/ Tel. +61 (3) 9650-1578
Newcastle — Govinda's Vegetarian Cafe, 110 King St., corner of King & Wolf Streets, NSW 2300/ Tel. +61 (2) 4929-6900 / info@

govindascafe.com.au
Perth — Hare Krishna Food for Life, 200 William St., Northbridge, WA 6003/ Tel. +61 (8) 9227-1684/ iskconperth@optusnet.com.au

NEW ZEALAND AND FIJI

Auckland, NZ — The Loft, 1st Floor, 103 Beach Rd./ Tel. +64 (9) 3797301
Christchurch, NZ — 83 Bealey Ave. (mail: P.O. Box 25-190)/ Tel. +64 (3) 366-5174/ Fax: +64 (3) 366-1965/ iskconchch@clear.net.nz
Hamilton, NZ — 188 Maui St., RD 8, Te Rapa/ Tel. +64 (7) 850-5108/ rmaster@wave.co.nz
Labasa, Fiji — Delailabasa (mail: P.O. Box 133)/ Tel. +679 812912
Lautoka, Fiji — 5 Tavewa Ave. (mail: P.O. Box 125)/ Tel. +679 666 4112/ regprakash@excite.com
Nausori, Fiji — Hare Krishna Cultural Centre, 2nd Floor, Shop & Save Building 11 Gulam Nadi St., Nausori Town (mail: P.O. Box 2183, Govt. Bldgs., Suva)/ Tel. +679 9969748 or 3475097/ Fax: +679 3477436/ vdas@frca.org.fj
Rakiraki, Fiji — Rewasa (mail: P.O. Box 204)/ Tel. +679 694243
Sigatoka, Fiji — Queens Rd., Olosara (mail: P.O. Box 1020)/ Tel. +679 6520866 or 6500349/ drgsmarna@connect.com.fj
Suva, Fiji — 166 Brewster St. (mail: P.O. Box 4229, Samabula)/ Tel. +679 331 8441/ Fax: +679 3100016/ iskconsuva@connect.com.fj
Wellington, NZ — 105 Newlands Rd., Newlands/ Tel. +64 (4) 478-4108/ info@iskconwellington.org.nz
Wellington, NZ — Gaura Yoga Centre, 1st Floor, 175 Vivian St. (mail: P.O. Box 6271, Marion Square)/ Tel. +64 (4) 801-5500/ yoga@gaurayoga.co.nz

RURAL COMMUNITY

Auckland, NZ (New Varshan) — Hwy. 28, Riverhead, next to Huapai Golf Course (mail: R.D. 2, Kumeu)/ Tel. +64 (9) 412-8075/ Fax: +64 (9) 412-7130

RESTAURANTS

Auckland, NZ — Hare Krishna Food for Life, 268 Karangahape Rd./ Tel. +64 (9) 300-7585
Labasa, Fiji — Hare Krishna Restaurant, Naseakula Road/ Tel. +679 811364
Lautoka, Fiji — Gopal's, Corner of Yasawa Street and Naviti Street/ Tel. +679 662990
Suva, Fiji — Hare Krishna Vegetarian Restaurant, Dolphins FNPF Place, Victoria Parade/ Tel. +679 314154/ vdas@govnet.gov.fj
Suva, Fiji — Hare Krishna Vegetarian Restaurant, Opposite University of the South Pacific, Laucala Bay Rd./ Tel. +679 311683/ vdas@govnet.gov.fj
Suva, Fiji — Hare Krishna Vegetarian Restaurant, 18 Pratt St./ Tel. +679 314154
Suva, Fiji — Hare Krishna Vegetarian Restaurant, 82 Ratu Mara Rd., Samabula/ Tel. +679 386333
Suva, Fiji — Hare Krishna Vegetarian Restaurant, Terry Walk, Cumming St./ Tel. +679 312295
Wellington, NZ — Higher Taste Hare Krishna Restaurant, Old Bank Arcade, Ground Flr., Corner Customhouse, Quay & Hunter St., Wellington/ Tel. +64 (4) 472-2233/ Fax: (4) 472-2234/ highertaste@iskconwellington.orgorg.nz

INDIA (partial list)*

Ahmedabad, Gujarat — Satellite Rd., Gandhinagar Highway Crossing, 380 054/ Tel. (079) 686-1945, -1645, or -2350/ jasomatinandan.acbsp@pamho.net
Allahabad, UP — Hare Krishna Dham, 161 Kashi Raj Nagar, Baluaghat 211 003/ Tel. (0532) 415294
Amritsar, Punjab — Chowk Moni Bazar, Laxmansar, 143 001/ Tel. (0183) 2540177
Bangalore, Karnataka — Hare Krishna Hill, Chord Rd., 560 010/ Tel. (080) 23471956 or 23578346/ Fax: (080) 23578625/ manjunath36@iskconbangalore.org
Bangalore, Karnataka — ISKCON Sri Jagannath Mandir, No.5 Sripuram, 1st cross, Sheshadripuram, Bangalore 560 020/ Tel. (080) 3536867 or 2262024 or 3530102
Baroda, Gujarat — Hare Krishna Land, Gotri Rd., 390 021/ Tel. (0265) 2310630 or 2331012/ iskcon.baroda@pamho.net
• **Bhubaneswar, Orissa** — N.H. No. 5, IRC Village, 751 015/ Tel. (0674) 2553517, 2553475, or 2554283
Chandigarh, Punjab — Hare Krishna Dham, Sector 36-B, 160 036/ Tel. (0172) 601590 or 603232/ iskcon.chandigarh@pamho.net
Chennai (Madras), TN — Hare Krishna Land, Bhaktivedanta Swami Road, Off ECR Road, Injam- bakkam, Chennai 600 041/ Tel. (044) 5019303 or 5019147/ iskconchennai@eth.net
• **Coimbatore, TN** — Jagannath Mandir, Hare Krishna Land, Aerodrome P.O., Opp. CIT, 641 014/ Tel. (0422) 2626509 or 2626508/ info@iskcon-coimbatore.org
Dwarka, Gujarat — Bharatiya Bhavan, Devi Bhavan Rd., 361 335/ Tel. (02892) 34606/ Fax: (02892) 34319
Guwahati, Assam — Ulubari Chariali, South Sarania, 781 007/ Tel. (0361) 2525963/ iskcon.guwahati@pamho.net
Haridwar, Uttaranchal — Prabhupada Ashram, G. House, Nai Basti, Mahadev Nagar, Bhimgoda/ Tel. (01334) 260818
Hyderabad, AP — Hare Krishna Land, Nampally Station Rd., 500 001/ Tel. (040) 24744969 or 24607089/ iskcon.hyderabad@pamho.net
Imphal, Manipur — Hare Krishna Land, Airport Rd., 795 001/ Tel. (0385) 2455245 or 2455247 or 2455693/ manimandir@sancharnet.in
Indore, MP — ISKCON, Nipania, Indore/ Tel. 9300474043/ mahaman.acbsp@pamho.net
Jaipur, Rajasthan — ISKCON Road, Opp. Vijay Path, Mansarovar, Jaipur 302 020 (mail: ISKCON, 84/230, Sant Namdev Marg, Opp. K.V. No. 5, Mansarovar, Jaipur 302 020)/ Tel. (0414) 2782765 or 2781860/ jaipur@pamho.net
Jammu, J&K — Srila Prabhupada Ashram, c/o Shankar Charitable Trust, Shakti Nagar, Near AG Office/ Tel. (01991) 233047
Kolkata (Calcutta), WB — 3C Albert Rd., 700 017 (behind Minto Park, opp. Birla High School)/ Tel. (033) 3028-9258 or -9280/ iskcon.calcutta@pamho.net
• **Kurukshetra, Haryana** — 369 Gudri Muhalla, Main Bazaar, 132 118/ Tel. (01744) 234806
Lucknow, UP — 1 Ashok Nagar, Guru Govind Singh Marg, 226 018/ Tel. (0522) 223556 or 271551
• **Mayapur, WB** — ISKCON, Shree Mayapur Chandrodaya Mandir, Shree Mayapur Dham, Dist. Nadia, 741 313/ Tel. (03472) 245239, 245240, or 245233/ Fax: (03472) 245238/ mayapur.chandrodaya@pamho.net
• **Mumbai (Bombay), Maharashtra** — Hare Krishna Land, Juhu 400 049/ Tel. (022) 26206860/ Fax: (022) 26205214/ info@iskconmumbai.com; guest.house.bombay@pamho.net
• **Mumbai, Maharashtra** — 7 K. M. Munshi Marg, Chowpatty 400 007 / Tel. (022) 23665500/ Fax: (022) 23665555/ info@radhagopinath.com
Mumbai, Maharashtra — Shristhi Complex, Mira Rd. (E), opposite Royal College, Dist. Thane, 401 107/ Tel. (022) 28454667 or 28454672/ Fax: (022) 28454981/ jagjivan.gkg@pamho.net
Mysore, Karnataka — #31, 18th Cross, Jayanagar, 570 014/ Tel. (0821) 2500582 or 6567333/ mysore.iskcon@gmail.com
Nellore, AP — ISKCON City, Hare Krishna Rd., 524 004/ Tel. (0861) 2314577 or (092155) 36589/ sukadevaswami@gmail.com
• **New Delhi, UP** — Hare Krishna Hill, Sant Nagar Main Road, East of Kailash, 110 065/ Tel. (011) 2623-5133, 4, 5, 6, 7/ Fax: (011) 2621-

5421/ delhi@pamho.net; (Guesthouse) neel.sunder@pamho.net
• **New Delhi, UP** — 41/77, Punjabi Bagh (West), 110 026/ Tel. (011) 25222851 or 25227478 Noida, UP — A-5, Sector 33, opp. NTPC office, Noida 201 301/ Tel. (0120) 2506211/ vraja.bhakti.vilas.lok@pamho.net
Patna, Bihar — Arya Kumar Rd., Rajendra Nagar, 800 016/ Tel. (0612) 687637 or 685081/ Fax: (0612) 687635/ krishna.kripa.jps@pamho.net
Pune, Maharashtra — 4 Tarapoor Rd., Camp, 411 001/ Tel. (020) 26332328 or 26361855/ iyfpune@vsnl.com
Puri, Orissa — Bhakti Kuti, Swargadwar, 752 001/ Tel. (06752) 231440 Raipur, Chhatisgarh — Hare Krishna Land, Alopi Nagar, Opposite Maharshi Vidyalaya, Tatibandh, Raipur 492 001/ Tel. (0771) 5037555/ iskconraipur@yahoo.com
Secunderabad, AP — 27 St. John's Rd., 500 026/ Tel. (040) 780-5232/ Fax: (040) 814021
Silchar, Assam — Ambikapatti, Silchar, Dist. Cachar, 788 004/ Tel. (03842) 34615
Sri Rangam, TN — 103 Amma Mandapam Rd., Sri Rangam, Trichy 620 006/ Tel. (0431) 2433945/ iskcon_srirangam@yahoo.com.in
Surat, Gujarat — Rander Rd., Jahangirpura, 395 005/ Tel. (0261) 765891, 765516, or 773386/ surat@pamho.net
• **Thiruvananthapuram (Trivandrum), Kerala** — Hospital Rd., Thycaud, 695 014/ Tel. (0471) 2328197/ jsdasa@yahoo.co.in
• **Tirupati, AP** — K.T. Rd., Vinayaka Nagar, 517 507/ Tel. (0877) 2230114 or 2230009/ revati.raman.jps@pamho.net (guesthouse: iskcon_ashram@yahoo.co.in)
Udhampur, J&K — Srila Prabhupada Ashram, Srila Prabhupada Marg, Srila Prabhupada Nagar 182 101/ Tel. (01992) 270298/ info@iskconudhampur.com
Ujjain, MP — Hare Krishna Land, Bharatpuri, 456 010/ Tel. (0734) 2535000 or 3205000/ Fax: (0734) 2536000/ iskcon.ujjain@pamhho.net
Varanasi, UP — ISKCON, B 27/80 Durgakund Rd., Near Durgakund Police Station, Varanasi 221 010/ Tel. (0542) 246422 or 222617
• **Vrindavan, UP** — Krishna-Balaram Mandir, Bhaktivedanta Swami Marg, Raman Reti, Mathura Dist., 281 124/ Tel. & Fax: (0565) 2540728/ iskcon.vrindavan@pamho.net; (Guesthouse:) Tel. (0565) 2540022; ramamani@sancharnet.in

ADDITIONAL RESTAURANT

Kolkata, WB — Govinda's, ISKCON House, 22 Gurusaday Rd., 700 019/ Tel. (033) 24756922, 24749009

EUROPE (partial list)*

Amsterdam — Van Hilligaertstraat 17, 1072 JX/ Tel. +31 (020) 675-1404 or -1694/ Fax: +31 (020) 675-1405/ amsterdam@pamho.net
Barcelona — Plaza Reial 12, Entlo 2, 08002/ Tel. +34 93 302-5194/ templobcn@hotmail.com
Bergamo, Italy — Villaggio Hare Krishna (da Medolago strada per Terno d'Isola), 24040 Chignolo d'Isola (BG)/ Tel. +39 (035) 4940706
Budapest — Lehel Street 15–17, 1039 Budapest/ Tel. +36 (01) 391-0435/ Fax: (01) 397-5219/ nai@pamho.net
Copenhagen — Skjulhoj Alle 44, 2720 Vanlose, Copenhagen/ Tel. +45 4828 6446/ Fax: +45 4828 7331/ iskcon.denmark@pamho.net
Grödinge, Sweden — Radha-Krishna Temple, Korsnäs Gård, 14792 Grödinge, Tel.+46 (08) 53029800/ Fax: +46 (08) 53025062 / bmd@pamho.net
Helsinki — Ruoholahdenkatu 24 D (III krs) 00180/ Tel. +358 (9) 694-9879 or -9837
• **Lisbon** — Rua Dona Estefânia, 91 R/C 1000 Lisboa/ Tel. & fax: +351(01) 314-0314 or 352-0038
Madrid — Espíritu Santo 19, 28004 Madrid/ Tel. +34 91 521-3096
Paris — 35 Rue Docteur Jean Vaquier, 93160 Noisy le Grand/ Tel. & fax: +33 (01) 4303-0951/ param.gati.swami@pamho.net
Prague — Jilova 290, Prague 5 - Zlicin 155 21/ Tel. +42 (02) 5795-0391/ info@harekrsna.cz
• **Radhadesh, Belgium** — Chateau de Petite Somme, 6940 Septon-Durbuy/ Tel. +32 (086) 322926 (restaurant: 321421)/ Fax: +32 (086) 322929/ radhadesh@pamho.net
• **Rome** — Govinda Centro Hare Krsna, via di Santa Maria del Pianto 16, 00186/ Tel. +39 (06) 68891540/ govinda.roma@harekrsna.it
• **Stockholm** — Fridhemsgatan 22, 11240/ Tel. +46 (08) 654-9002/ Fax: +46 (08) 650-881; Restaurant: Tel. & fax: +46 (08) 654-9004/ lokanatha@hotmail.com
Warsaw — Mysiadlo k. Warszawy, 05-500 Piaseczno, ul. Zakret 11/ Tel. +48 (022) 750-7797 or -8247/ Fax: +48 (022) 750-8249/ kryszna@post.pl
Zürich — Bergstrasse 54, 8030/ Tel. +41 (01) 262-3388/ Fax: +41 (01) 262-3114/ kgs@pamho.net

RURAL COMMUNITIES

France (La Nouvelle Mayapura) — Domaine d'Oublaisse, 36360, Lucay le Mâle/ Tel. +33 (02) 5440-2395/ Fax: +33 (02) 5440-2823/ oublaise@free.fr
Germany (Simhachalam) — Zielberg 20, 94118 Jandelsbrunn/ Tel. +49 (08583) 316/ info@simhachalam.de
Hungary (New Vraja-dhama) — Krisna-völgy, 8699 Somogyvamos, Fö u, 38/ Tel. & fax: +36 (085) 540-002 or 340-185/ info@krisnavolgy.hu
Italy (Villa Vrindavan) — Via Scopeti 108, 50026 San Casciano in Val di Pesa (FL)/ Tel. +39 (055) 820054/ Fax: +39 (055) 828470/ isvaripriya@libero.it
Spain (New Vraja Mandala) — (Santa Clara) Brihuega, Guadalajara/ Tel. +34 949 280436

ADDITIONAL RESTAURANTS

Barcelona — Restaurante Govinda, Plaza de la Villa de Madrid 4–5, 08002/ Tel. +34 (93) 318-7729
Copenhagen — Govinda's, Nørre Farimagsgade 82, DK-1364 Kbh K/ Tel. +45 3333 7444
Milan — Govinda's, Via Valpetrosa 5, 20123/ Tel. +39 (02) 862417
Oslo — Krishna's Cuisine, Kirkeveien 59B, 0364/ Tel. +47 (02) 260-6250
Zürich — Govinda Veda-Kultur, Preyergrasse 16, 8001/ Tel. & fax: +41 (01) 251-8859/ info@govinda-shop.ch

CIS (partial list)*

Kiev — 16, Zorany per., 04078/ Tel. +380 (044) 433-8312, or 434-7028 or -5533
Moscow — 8/3, Khoroshevskoye sh. (mail: P.O. Box 69), 125284/ Tel. +7 (095) 255-6711/ Tel. & fax: +7 (095) 945-3317

ASIA (partial list)*

Bangkok, Thailand — Soi3, Tanon Itsarapap, Toonburi/ Tel. +66 (02) 9445346 or (081) 4455401 or (089) 7810623/ swami.bvv.narasimha@pamho.net
Dhaka, Bangladesh — 5 Chandra Mohon Basak St., Banagram,1203/ Tel. +880 (02) 236249/ Fax: (02) 837287/ iskcon_bangladesh@yahoo.com
Hong Kong — 6/F Oceanview Court, 27 Chatham Road South (mail: P.O. Box 98919)/ Tel. +852 (2) 739-6818/ Fax: +852 (2) 724-2186/ iskcon.hong.kong@pamho.net
Jakarta, Indonesia — Yayasan Radha-Govinda, P.O. Box 2694, Jakarta Pusat 10001/ Tel. +62 (021) 489-9646/ matsyads@bogor.wasantara.net.id
Katmandu, Nepal — Budhanilkantha (mail: GPO Box 3520)/ Tel.

+977 (01) 373790 or 373786/ Fax: +977 (01) 372976 (Attn: ISKCON)/ iskcon@wlink.com.np

Kuala Lumpur, Malaysia — Lot 9901, Jalan Awan Jawa, Taman Yarl, 58200 Kuala Lumpur/ Tel. +60 (3) 7980-7355/ Fax: +60 (3) 7987-9901/ president@iskconkl.com

Manila, Philippines — Radha-Madhava Center, #9105 Banuyo St., San Antonio village, Makati City/ Tel. +63 (02) 8963357; Tel. & fax: +63 (02) 8901947/ iskconmanila@yahoo.com

Myitkyina, Myanmar — ISKCON Sri Jagannath Temple, Bogyoke Street, Shansu Taung, Myitkyina, Kachin State/ mahanadi@mptmail.net.mm

Tai Pei City, Taiwan — Ting Zhou Rd. Section 3, No. 192, 4F, Tai Pei City 100/ Tel. +886 (02) 2365-8641/ dayal.nitai.tkg@pamho.net

Tokyo, Japan — Subaru 1F, 4-19-6 Kamitakada, Nakano-ku, Tokyo 164-0002/ Tel. +81 (03) 5343- 9147 or (090) 6544-9284/ Fax: +81 (03) 5343-3812/ damodara@krishna.jp

LATIN AMERICA (partial list)*

Buenos Aires, Argentina — Centro Bhaktivedanta, Andonaegui 2054, Villa Urquiza, CP 1431/ Tel. +54 (01) 523-4232/ Fax: +54 (01) 523-8085/ iskcon-ba@gopalnet.com

Caracas, Venezuela — Av. Los Proceres (con Calle Marquez del Toro), San Bernardino/ Tel. +58 (212) 550-1818

Guayaquil, Ecuador — 6 de Marzo 226 and V. M. Rendon/ Tel. +593 (04) 308412 or 309420/ Fax: +564 302108/ gurumani@gu.pro.ec

• **Lima, Peru** — Schell 634 Miraflores/ Tel. +51 (014) 444-2871

Mexico City, Mexico — Tiburcio Montiel 45, Colonia San Miguel, Chapultepec D.F., 11850/ Tel. +52 (55) 5273-1953/ Fax: +52 (55) 52725944

Rio de Janeiro, Brazil — Rua Vilhena de Morais, 309, Barra da Tijuca, 22793-140/ Tel. +55 (021) 2491-1887/ sergio.carvalho@pobox.com

San Salvador, El Salvador — Calle Chiltiupan #39, Ciudad Merliot, Nueva San Salvador (mail: A.P. 1506)/ Tel. +503 2278-7613/ Fax: +503 2229-1472/ tulasikrishnadas@yahoo.com

São Paulo, Brazil — Rua do Paraiso, 694, 04103-000/Tel. +55 (011) 326-0975/ communicacaomandir@grupos.com.br

West Coast Demerara, Guyana — Sri Gaura Nitai Ashirvad Mandir, Lot "B," Nauville Flanders (Crane Old Road), West Coast Demerara/ Tel. +592 254 0494/ iskcon.guyana@yahoo.com

AFRICA (partial list)*

Accra, Ghana — Samsam Rd., Off Accra-Nsawam Hwy., Medie, Accra North (mail: P.O. Box 11686)/ Tel. & fax +233 (021) 229988/ srivas_bts@yahoo.co.in

Cape Town, South Africa — 17 St. Andrews Rd., Rondebosch 7700/ Tel. +27 (021) 6861179/ Fax: +27 (021) 686-8233/ cape.town@pamho.net

• **Durban, South Africa** — 50 Bhaktivedanta Swami Circle, Unit 5 (mail: P.O. Box 56003), Chatsworth, 4030/ Tel. +27 (031) 403-3328/ Fax: +27 (031) 403-4429/ iskcon.durban@pamho.net

Johannesburg, South Africa — 7971 Capricorn Ave. (entrance on Nirvana Drive East), Ext. 9, Lenasia (mail: P.O. Box 926, Lenasia 1820)/ Tel. +27 (011) 854-1975 or 7969/ iskconjh@iafrica.com

Lagos, Nigeria — 12, Gani Williams Close, off Osolo Way, Ajao Estate, International Airport Rd. (mail: P.O. Box 8793, Marina)/ Tel. +234 (01) 7744926 or 7928906/ bdds.bts@pamho.net

Mombasa, Kenya — Hare Krishna House, Sauti Ya Kenya and Kisumu Rds. (mail: P.O. Box 82224, Mombasa)/ Tel. +254 (011) 312248

Nairobi, Kenya — Muhuroni Close, off West Nagara Rd. (mail: P.O. Box 28946)/ Tel. +254 (203) 744365/ Fax: +254 (203) 740957/ iskcon_nairobi@yahoo.com

• **Phoenix, Mauritius** — Hare Krishna Land, Pont Fer (mail: P.O. Box 108, Quartre Bornes)/ Tel. +230 696-5804/ Fax: +230 696-8576/ iskcon.hkl@intnet.mu

Port Harcourt, Nigeria — Umuebule 11, 2nd tarred road, Etche (mail: P.O. Box 4429, Trans Amadi)/ Tel. +234 08033215096/ canakyaus@yahoo.com

Pretoria, South Africa — 1189 Church St., Hatfield, 0083 (mail: P.O. Box 14077, Hatfield, 0028)/ Tel. & fax: +27 (12) 342-6216/ iskconpt@global.co.za

RURAL COMMUNITY

Mauritius (ISKCON Vedic Farm) — Hare Krishna Rd., Vrindaban/ Tel. +230 418-3185 or 418-3955/ Fax: +230 418-6470

***The full list is always available at Krishna.com, where it also includes Krishna conscious gatherings.**

Far from a Center? Call us at 1-800-927-4152. Or contact us on the Internet
http://www.krishna.com • E-mail: bbt.usa@krishna.com

BHAGAVAD-GĪTĀ AS IT IS

The world's most popular edition of a timeless classic.

Throughout the ages, the world's greatest minds have turned to the *Bhagavad-gītā* for answers to life's perennial questions. Renowned as the jewel of India's spiritual wisdom, the *Gītā*

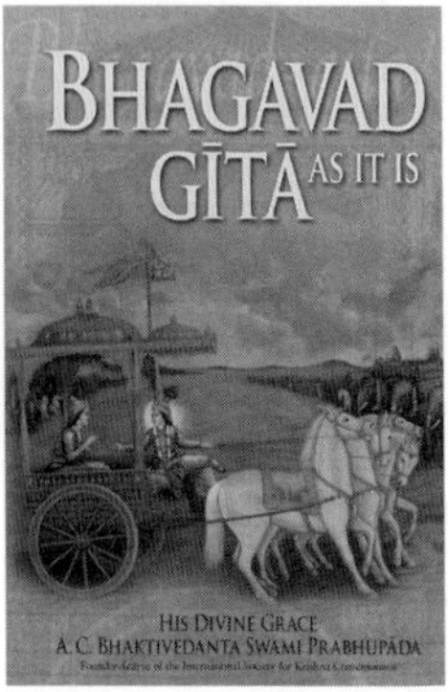

summarizes the profound Vedic knowledge concerning man's essential nature, his environment, and ultimately his relationship with God. With more than fifty million copies sold in twenty languages, *Bhagavad-gītā As It Is*, by His Divine Grace A.C. Bhaktivedanta Swami Prabhupāda, is the most widely read edition of the *Gītā* in the world. It includes the original Sanskrit text, phonetic transliterations, word-for-word meanings, translation, elaborate commentary, and many full-color illustrations. (Pocket version: translation and commentary only.)

Pocket	Vinyl	Hard	Deluxe
$4.50	$8.50	$9.95	$19.95
BGS	BGV	BGH	BGD

ORDER TOLL FREE 1-800-927-4152